CAN I STAY IN THE CATHOLIC CHURCH?

The Church, the mystical Body of Christ, has become a monstrosity. The head is very large, but the body is shrunken.

Alex Carter's summary of a talk given by Pope Pius XI in 1939 to a group of Canadian students

Brian Lennon SJ

Can I Stay in the Catholic Church?

the columba press

First published in 2012 by
the columba press
55A Spruce Avenue, Stillorgan Industrial Park,
Blackrock, Co Dublin

Cover by Bill Bolger
Origination by The Columba Press
Printed by Colorman Limited, Ireland

ISBN 978-1-85607-753 8

Contents

Can I stay in the Catholic Church?

Two images are useful starting points for this book.

The first was an email from my brother on 19 April 2005 telling me that there was white smoke at the Vatican. I was surprised. The conclave to elect a new Pope had started only a few days before. I had told myself I was not interested: the outcome would not have a great impact on the church.

Besides, given the negotiations that go on within a conclave I expected it to be at least a week before a new Pope was elected. But a glance at a news site confirmed my brother's email and I knew that this meant only one thing: Joseph Ratzinger had been elected. I turned on the TV and was greeted by the sight of the Cardinals standing together in all their robes on one of the balconies in St Peters, waving to the crowds and smiling happily.

As Prefect for the Congregation for the Doctrine of the Faith Cardinal Ratzinger had held an important role in the long papacy of John Paul II. He represented continuity with John Paul. For many that was good news, but for me it was bad, in terms of John Paul's internal policies, as distinct from his work in Eastern Europe, Jewish-Christian relations and other areas. There was much about the church's internal government that I felt was wrong. Continuity meant that this was to continue. As it turned out there would also be much that I was to appreciate in the new Pope.

The second image was the Ryan Report (2009) into the abuse of children in institutions run by religious in Ireland. It revealed in graphic detail some of the suffering of the children. It also showed just how many of them there were and how their suffering had continued over years. It showed also that the failure by church authorities to respond was widespread and systemic.

These two images raised a question for me: can I remain a Catholic? This question was not new. The urgency of it was. Three groups of issues lay behind it. Unless I could deal with each of these the answer to the question would be No.

The first set of issues was about God: is there a God? If so, who is this God? It might seem surprising that after 40 years of life as a Jesuit that I might still be wondering if there is a God.

Yet that wonder has, if anything, increased rather than diminished over the years. Paradoxically the question has deepened while at the same time my experience of the deep, silent presence of God has also deepened.

The second set of issues was about the structures of the church. This has been a long-term problem for me, even before the abuse crisis: why is the church so clericalist? Why are lay people excluded from authority? What lies behind the ban on the ordination of married people and women? How is it that lay people are expected to accept teaching and other decisions when they have played no role in their formulation?

The third issue – abuse – permeated the first two: the fact that so many children had been abused made it much harder to find God in the church. It also raised questions about our structures: did the particular structures that we had in the church make the bad response to abuse more likely? Are the values behind these structures connected with the response to it? How could church authorities act as they did? What did they know about abuse and its dynamics? Why did they move known abusers from one place to another where their abuse continued? Why were so many children abused instead of being protected by an institution whose only purpose is to image the love of God in the world?

The airwaves were full of accusations against the church as a whole; except that the church they were talking about was not the church as a whole. Rather it was the Pope, bishops, clergy and religious.

That included me. But why me? What wrong had I done? Was I tied into this horror? Did I contribute to the culture that helped make the response to the abuse so bad? In turn these questions led to others: was it only the clergy and religious who created the culture? Did lay people make some contribution to it?

When I began writing this book it seemed clear to me that failing to come up with satisfactory answers to these questions would make it impossible to stay in the church. Obviously if I concluded that there is no God then the church is pointless. Secondly, if church structures are not only corrupt but irredeemably so, then the search for God needs to take place in some other institution.

To tackle the issues in the book I look first at abuse within the church: what happened and who was to blame? I argue that those church leaders who made wrong decisions clearly bear much of the responsibility, but others are involved because of corporate connectedness, something quite different from personal guilt. The question this raises is: are some lay people, as well as clergy, involved?

I also wanted to examine the way people explained why the abuse happened and the response to it. Further, was the culture of the time an influence? If so, in what way? What particular aspects of it made abuse of children and the secretive response to it more likely?

In the second section I look at the question of God: one part of this is a personal exploration of how secularism challenges me. These challenges have been and are real. This is not surprising given that so much of Western culture has difficulty imagining a world beyond the visible and measurable. Yet all our lives are dominated by relationships which can never be measured.

The second part of this section goes back to parts of the scriptures which have led me to God. These two streams – secularism and the experience of God not only in the scriptures but also in my relationships and the topsy turvy of life – flow along within me, sometimes one dominant, sometimes the other. I suspect others experience similar paradoxes. In the light of this, can I believe in God?

In the third section I look at the church in scripture and tradition. There is a temptation for many, including myself, not to address issues of church. The church is about a community of believers and it is easier, much easier, to stay with questions about me and God, rather than moving on to the community.

Communities complicate things. They are awkward, disturbing, challenging, although they can also be comforting. Yet it is clear from the Christian scriptures that God calls us not only as individuals but also as a community. That was the experience of the Jewish people to whom Jesus belonged. It has also been our experience as followers of Christ.

The church is the Body of Christ. As the Body of Christ it is the principal means by which God is revealed through Christ in the world. We are called to be the sign of the presence of God in the world. Abuse and the response to it are the very antithesis of this. It is important to spell out the ideals that the church sets itself in order to show the appalling gap between these and the reality.

Not surprisingly the church has changed constantly since its earliest beginnings. The church we have now would feel strange in many ways to St Paul and his companions. What are the differences and the similarities between the church of Paul's time and ours? What continuity and discontinuity has there been? Which changes are possible that are in keeping with the scriptures and tradition, and which are not?

Finally, in the fifth section I ask is there any hope? My tentative answer is Yes, but it depends on repentance and that in turn depends on change.

In the conclusion I come back again to the question which is the title of the book: can I stay in the Catholic Church?

I have tried to make the book accessible to people with limited theological knowledge, first because I am not a theologian, and secondly, because at root the question of what church we belong to impacts deeply on our relationship with God. It is therefore a deeply personal question. Yet it was also necessary to explore the scriptures and history of the church because these reveal values that are important in the church and at times also show how we have moved away from our basic vision.

Exploring the issue of whether or not to stay in the church has not been easy, but it is an issue with which thousands of Catholics all over the world are struggling. I have found it helpful to go back to our sources, to be reminded again of the passionate love God has for us, of times past when the People of God have wandered from the Way of God's call to repentance and the ultimate guarantee of God's forgiveness.

This has also helped to highlight changes that the church has to make.

The only Christian response that we as a sinful church can make to the wrongdoing of the institution and to our own personal sins is to repent.

Being a Catholic today for many is a peculiar experience. On the one hand we are given the extraordinary gift of learning about and experiencing Our Lord through the scriptures, in the sacraments and especially in the Eucharist. On the other we are part of a church in which some officials have carried out horrifying abuse which was not responded to properly. As well, many of our structures would not survive even a cursory examination based on human rights standards. Further, all of us as individuals are sinners, so we cannot be self-righteous in condemning others.

There have been many times in the past when the People of God, or God's Chosen People in the Old Testament, were found wanting when faced with the judgement of God. That judgement was not that of an angry beast determined to destroy the people, but rather the consequences people and groups brought on themselves by separating themselves from a loving, compassionate God. We live in such times today.

I have found it helpful for myself to look at these issues and I hope others may find the book useful in their own reflections. But first it is important to remind ourselves about what actually happened to the children who suffered.

SECTION ONE

Abuse In The Catholic Church

CHAPTER ONE

What Happened?

1. *The Ryan and Murphy Reports*

In 2009 the Ryan and Murphy reports exposed an horrendous story of extensive abuse of young people in the care of institutions in Ireland run by religious orders, and also of abuse by some Dublin diocesan priests. What was more shocking was that the reports showed religious superiors and bishops often protected abusers from the law which led to further abuse. It is worth referring to part of these reports to remind ourselves of the horrors involved.

The Ryan Report gives a flavour of what the young people went through:

Witnesses said that they were hit, beaten, flogged, kicked and otherwise physically assaulted, scalded, burned and held under water. They were beaten in front of other staff, residents, patients and pupils as well as in private. Many reported broken bones, lacerations and bruising as a result of beatings.

Sexual abuse 'was endemic in boys' institutions', although not in girls' schools. 'Acute and chronic contact and non-contact sexual abuse was reported, including vaginal and anal rape, molestation and voyeurism in both isolated assaults and on a regular basis over long periods of time.'

'Female witnesses in particular described, at times, being told they were responsible for the sexual abuse they experienced, by both their abuser and those to whom they disclosed abuse.'

They suffered emotional abuse: 'lack of attachment and affection, loss of identity, deprivation of family contact, humiliation, constant criticism, personal denigration, exposure to fear and the threat of harm. A frequently identified area of emotional abuse was the separation from siblings and loss of family contact. Witnesses were incorrectly told their parents were dead and were given false information about their siblings and family members. Many witnesses recalled the devastating emotional impact and feeling of powerlessness associated with observing their co-residents, siblings or others being abused. This trauma was acute for those who were forced to participate in such incidents'.

These abuses were known to those in charge and their response was either to do nothing or to move the abusers to other situations where more abuse was carried out.

The church is the Body of Christ. It is meant to be the visible sign of the presence of God in the world, to show the compassion, the forgiveness, the justice, the hope that God holds out to all people. It always fails in that goal because it is a human institution. Those failures make it harder for it to fulfil its task because instead of being a sign of God's love it becomes a block to people experiencing that love. Never was this more true than in the crisis over child sexual abuse by clergy and religious.

The Body of Christ is also the bodies of children who were abused.

2. The voice of a victim

We need to analyse the causes and effects of child abuse by clerics and religious. It is not easy to do this because of our horror at what is involved. Nonetheless analysis is important. Otherwise the danger is that our anger can block us from identifying the deeper issues and possible ways forward. As part of this analysis it is important at all times to keep in mind what it is that the children suffered. The following piece by Andrew Madden, who was abused by Fr Ivan Payne, shows the pain more graphically because he is describing what he himself experienced:

> I remember both my anger and sadness rising as I sat in offices of the Department of Justice early one morning a year ago reading about the nine-year-old girl who had to experience a priest put his hands inside her trousers during confession so as to abuse her, washing his hands in an altar bowl afterwards. I felt sad for the boys who had to endure a priest's predilection for 'corporal punishment', which gardaí subsequently described as brutal and having sado-sexual connotations.
>
> I felt sad for the boys who were taken on holiday by 'Fr Dante' and who were subject to his rules that all the boys were to sleep naked, that the bathroom door was to be left

open when they were showering, that 'punishment' was to be smacking on the bare bottom and that a different boy had to sleep with the priest every night. I felt sad for the boys who were sexually abused by Fr McNamee having been attracted to the indoor and outdoor swimming pools at his parochial house in Crumlin, which adults were excluded from using.

I was angry that another priest had sexually abused one boy while taking photographs at the same time and was so aggressive with another boy that he knocked him unconscious. On subsequently moving to the diocese of San Diego, he received a reference from Archbishop Connell to the effect that he was 'an excellent priest in many ways' and 'a priest in good standing'. I was angry that another priest, against whom allegations of child sexual abuse had already been made, was appointed chaplain to a school for deaf children, and that the first complaint against him there was made within a month of that appointment. This was a priest who kissed girls in confession and rubbed his hands all over their bodies inside their clothing. I was angry that despite these complaints he remained a curate in a parish for another four years.

I was angry that Fr Payne had been left in a position to sexually abuse at least seven more boys after I had told the archdiocese of Dublin about him in 1981.

As I mark the anniversary of the publication of the Murphy report, I think about the awfulness of what so many children endured and I wonder how they coped with what was happening to them. I wonder too about how their lives have been affected since; did they survive? Did they ever find happiness? How are they now?

I think about my own childhood experiences as an 11- or 12-year-old boy with Fr Ivan Payne. He had asked me to his house after serving 8am Mass during the school summer holidays; he said it was his way of saying thank you. Instead over time he got me into a pattern of going down to his house on a regular basis where he molested me as we sat on his couch watching television. I was so glad of that television; I had something to focus on while he did what he wanted. I froze. I didn't acknowledge what he was doing in any way shape or form. I didn't want to and I didn't know how to. Rarely did he. My way of coping was to keep my eyes on the television. I remember on one early occasion I got up from the couch and went upstairs to the bathroom. When I came back downstairs and walked into the sitting room I could have sat in any other chair away from him. But I didn't. I couldn't. That would have been to acknowledge what he had been doing and I felt completely unable to do that. I sat right back down beside him. He didn't need to use any harsh words or violent acts to control me. His position as a priest of our parish and the grooming he had initially engaged in were enough to secure my compliance. I was never going to tell anyone either. He knew that too. What words would I use? Who could ever believe what I would have to tell them? Everyone would know what I had been involved in, which is how I saw it at the time.

In the months leading up to my Junior Cert I felt strong enough to tell Fr Payne I wasn't coming to his house anymore, I needed to study. Over the next couple of years I did my best to put the past behind me but it was impossible.

I felt very bad about myself on every level. I felt unattractive. I didn't like my body. I covered up as much as I could, often wearing too many clothes during the summer when jeans and a T-shirt would have done. I didn't join in sport at school. I felt far too inhibited. I would never have felt free enough to run down to a basketball court or play football.

Worst of all I felt I had let Fr Payne do things that no other boy in class would have allowed. As an adult I can look back and see that's not how it was, but as a struggling teenager, such thoughts were crushing.

I noticed the boys in school and wondered about girls. When I was 17 or 18 I wanted to ask a particular girl out but I wasn't sure what she would expect me to do. I had some idea by then of what I might want to do but was this normal? Is it what other boys were doing? Or did I only know about such things because of my experiences with Fr Payne? If so, would she react badly and tell everyone?

At a time when I should have been throwing myself at every opportunity that presented itself, I withdrew, further compounding my feelings of isolation and loneliness.

Little wonder I found solace in alcohol and clumsily tried to overdose with tablets – all I really wanted was to let people know that I was hurting badly and couldn't cope, but I didn't know how to say it.

In my 20s, I had experiences and relationships with women and then with men. I'm sure the realisation that I was gay would have come to me a lot earlier if I had been left to grow up and develop in my own way and in my own time, free of Fr Payne's interference.

Over time with these experiences and relationships it became clear to me that I had great difficulty enjoying emotional and physical intimacy with the same person at the same time and I have always attributed that to my experiences with Fr Payne.

So years after the childhood sexual abuse had ended, its effects had me engaged in a pattern of behaviour which compounded the isolation and loneliness I had felt as a struggling teenager. Alcohol made that bearable but was doing its own damage.

When I first went public about those childhood experiences 15 years ago, I had no idea that my battles with church and state would be matched by a personal battle to look at what I had become and try to recover.

I think again about how many thousands of children suffered experiences like mine at the hands of priests whom Catholic bishops had covered up for over many decades.

Today, as those bishops (and the commentators who still minimise what they did and make excuses for them) bemoan how hard done by they feel at the media and public response to the Murphy report, I invite them to think about the enormous suffering caused to so many children simply because for those bishops the reputation of the church was more important.
Let it not be more important than the truth.[1]

In the light of the abuse and the response to it, Andrew Madden, understandably, left the church.

Who was to blame for the church's response to abuse? It is to that question that I now want to turn.

---

1. Andrew Madden, 'Murphy Report – One Year On', *Irish Times*, 25 November 2010.

CHAPTER TWO

Who was to Blame?

The church is the Body of Christ. It is meant to be the visible sign of the presence of God in the world, to show the compassion, the forgiveness, the justice, the hope that God holds out to all people. It always fails in that goal. Those failures make it harder for it to fulfil its task because instead of being a sign of God's love it becomes a block to people experiencing that love. Never was this more truly obvious than in the crisis over child sexual abuse by clergy and religious.

The Body of Christ is also the bodies of children who were abused.

Why was the church response so bad? Who was to blame?

(a) Who was to Blame: Bishops and Religious Superiors?

As mentioned already, the abuse crisis in 2009 was not new. There had been credible public reports of clerical abuse since at least the early 1990s. People had been shocked then. Yet the response to the Murphy and Ryan Reports was both deeper and more angry. This may have been because the reports pulled together the considerable number of cases, or because they spelled out in detail what was involved in the abuse, or because the stories of those who suffered got more space on the media. In any case clergy and religious as a whole, but especially bishops and superiors, were blamed for the failure to deal with the abuse.

Some of this was scapegoating. In the Old Testament, as part of their ceremonies of repentance, the community chose two goats. One was sacrificed to God. The other was driven out into the desert as a symbol of expelling the sins of the community (Leviticus 16). The goat was of course entirely innocent but it served a useful purpose: the community could move blame and responsibility from itself on to the goat.

But the abuse crisis was not simply about scapegoating innocent victims. Many individuals were guilty, the most obvious examples being the priests and religious who abused children. The second guilty group was the bishops and superiors who moved them into new situations where the abuse continued, if at that time the bishops or superiors knew of the addictive nature of abuse. One of the contested issues is to what extent they did in fact understand this aspect of abuse.

Secondly, it was not surprising that all priests and bishops were blamed by many for the crisis. Leaders – and others with little power – get blamed when organisations offend. For example, many see the Orange Order in Northern Ireland as a group opposed to the Catholic church. If I were an Orangeman, and if some Orangemen had been raping Catholic children for 30 years, and if some senior officers of the organisation had known about this and failed to stop it, then I would be unlikely to get a warm reception if I turned up at a meeting of Catholics to extol the virtues of the Orange Order. Another example is the way many blamed all bank workers for the financial crash in 2008-10.

How much was known about abuse at the time? The Ryan Report (Conclusion, 21) argues that the Congregations were aware of the addictive nature of abuse. Others dispute this.

Moira Higgins was a post-graduate social work student in University College Dublin in 1975. The degree for which she studied was a British qualification which certified her to practise in both the UK and in Ireland. While child protection was a concern, child sexual abuse was not even mentioned:

> There were no guidelines and no protocols, not even for professionals working for the health boards. If I had to deal with a case, which mercifully I did not, it would not have occurred to me to go to the Garda Síochána – and I was the health board representative.
>
> We were profoundly ignorant of the nature and extent of child sexual abuse and paedophilia. It was not talked about; it was not written about; victims did not speak out; they were not interviewed on radio. Thirty-five years on, knowing what we know now, that seems incredible, but it was true for me and I suspect it was true for most of my professional colleagues whose job it was to know these things. We were all truly ignorant and with what we know now there were terrible consequences. [1]

1. *Irish Times*, Letters, 20 March 2010.

It would not be surprising if bishops and religious superiors, most of whom were not trained social workers, shared a similar ignorance. Moira Higgins was commenting on the condemnation of Cardinal Sean Brady for failing as a priest in 1975 to report Fr Brendan Smyth to the police, although he believed the allegations against Fr Smyth were true. In fact the then Fr Brady reported the matter to his bishop, marked it for his urgent attention and strongly recommended that action be taken against Fr Smyth. Three weeks later the bishop withdrew Fr Smith's faculties to hear confession, reported the matter to his religious superior and left it to him to deal with it.

Calls for Cardinal Brady's resignation came because he did not report the matter to the police. By the standards of 2010 such calls were appropriate. But in the context of 1975 the then Fr Brady acted better than many of his contemporaries. He was neither a bishop nor a religious superior. In the light of Moira Higgins' letter his failure to report to the police is not surprising. Further, if he had done so it is quite likely that the police would not have taken appropriate action. Police, like the rest of society, acted with deference to clerics in the church.

Child sexual abuse became a public issue in the US only in the early 1970s and in the UK about ten years later, and even then its psychology and the appropriate response to it was not known.

So, in judging individuals do we apply the standards of the time, or those of 35 years later?

Bishops and congregational leaders also argued, not unreasonably, that they often sent men to mental health professionals who cleared them for further pastoral work. How could church leaders reasonably go against the advice of experts?

However, these arguments, while valid up to a point, have limits. The argument that a bishop or superior was not wrong to follow medical advice had merit the first time a person abused. It weakens drastically as more abuse occurs.

From 1987 on, church leaders took action to cover themselves financially by taking out insurance. This indicated that they were aware that cases were likely to go to court with the possibility of losing them.

From around that time the addictive nature of abuse was beginning to become clear to mental health professionals, so the
argument about lack of knowledge also weakens progressively
from then on.

Even before the addictive nature of abuse was known some
religious superiors had already treated lay offenders differently
from members of their congregations:

> Cases of sexual abuse were managed with a view to min-
> imising the risk of public disclosure and consequent damage
> to the institution and the Congregation ... When lay people
> were discovered to have sexually abused, they were generally
> reported to the Gardaí. When a member of a Congregation
> was found to be abusing, it was dealt with internally and
> was not reported to the Gardaí ... The desire to protect the
> reputation of the Congregation and institution was para-
> mount. *(Ryan, Conclusion 20).*

The issue of personal guilt and blame arises, then, when bishops
or superiors knew about abuse and its addictive nature and took
no action to protect children from the men or women over whom
they had authority. It also arises when they treated priests and
religious differently from lay people.

Bishops and religious in Ireland are part of the wider church.
A key leadership role in the wider church is taken by Popes and
the officials of the Vatican. What responsibility did they have?

(b) Who was to Blame: The Vatican?
The Vatican is implicated in the Irish abuse crisis. It must have
known for a long time about the abuse. (The files on sexual
abuse in Artane Industrial School in Dublin were known as the
'Rome' files [Chapter 7, *Ryan Report*]). They received frequent
reports from bishops and nuncios. All the bishops in Ireland
were appointed by the Pope. All were accountable to him. So
were the international heads of religious orders.

How much did the nuncios feed back to Rome? How much
were they aware of the inadequacies of the response of bishops
and congregational superiors? If they did not know, should they
have known?

The abuse crisis was international. In recent times it first surfaced in Canada, then in the US, and only later emerged in other countries. What steps could the Vatican have taken internationally, once the crisis was known about in one country? Should they not have looked more closely at the situation in other countries? This question is not only one of history: it applied in 2010. In what other countries in the world is clerical abuse still taking place? What investigative measures has the Vatican put in place? What structures of accountability have been set up? What measures have been taken to confront patriarchy? What protocols and training for child protection have been put in place?

Pope Benedict admitted that the Vatican 'addressed these things very slowly and late'.[1] He was referring to the case of Marcial Maciel, founder of the Legionaries of Christ, who was found guilty by the Vatican of abusing young boys for decades. 'Somehow', the Pope says, the matters 'were concealed very well, and only around the year 2000 did we have any concrete clues'. It would be six years later before the Vatican responded to this case by confining Maciel to a monastery. He remained a priest.

In 2002 Cardinal Castrillon Hoyos, head of the Congregation for the Clergy, congratulated French Bishop Pierre Pican for not informing the authorities about the crimes of one of his priests, Abbot Bissey. The latter served three months in prison. From Cardinal Hoyos' perspective Bishop Pican was correct in protecting his 'priest-son'. This comment revealed a central attitude of many in the Vatican: it was more important to give priority to the bishop-priest relationship than to protecting children. In theological terms the bishop is called to be a father of *all* the faithful.

The Irish bishops, when they started to respond to the problem, ran into problems with the Vatican. Bishop Michael Smith has spoken of the efforts of Cardinal Connell, Archbishop of Dublin, to have Tony Walsh, who abused numerous children, laicised. In 1990 he set up a canonical tribunal to try Bill Carney and in 1992 a second one to try Tony Walsh. The fact that these were among the first tribunals devoted to this issue itself shows how slow the church was to respond, even internally. The

---

1. Peter Seewald, *Light of the World*, quoted in *The Tablet*, 27 November 2010, p 10.

Murphy Report found that the archdiocese was aware of complaints against Tony Walsh from 1978. The tribunal found Walsh guilty and recommended that he be laicised. Walsh appealed to the Vatican and his sentence was reduced to being confined to a monastery. But the Cardinal could not find a monastery to take him. He then approached a senior member of the Curia in Rome and the priest was dismissed in January 1996.

Partly as a result of the Walsh case, the bishops and religious orders in Ireland produced new guidelines in 1996 which included a commitment to report 'serious' cases to the police. In 2011 a *Would You Believe* programme on RTÉ made public that in 1997 the Irish Bishops had received a letter from the then nuncio, Archbishop Luciano Storero, stating that the issue of mandatory reporting 'gives rise to serious concerns of both a moral and a canonical nature'. One unnamed bishop wrote of the meeting at which they were informed of this letter: 'We have received a mandate from the Congregation for the Clergy asking us to conceal the reported crimes of a priest.'

Bishop Michael Smith's response to the letter was that it would have been unhelpful to confront the Vatican publicly and instead they had to work quietly behind the scenes to persuade them to change their views.[1]

In fact the letter seems to have been part of a developing struggle within the Vatican about how to respond to the crisis. In 2010 Jeffrey Lena, who represents the Vatican in abuse cases in the US, said its main purpose 'was to help ensure that bishops who discipline their priests for sexual abuse did so in a manner that would ensure that the priest not avoid punishment based upon technical grounds' and that nowhere did the letter instruct Irish bishops not to report cases to the civil authorities. The letter was also written before John Paul II put Joseph Ratzinger, then in charge of the Congregation for the Doctrine of the Faith, in overall charge of the church's response.[2]

In 1998 Cardinal Hoyos met the Irish bishops and told them that Vatican policy was to protect the priest. The Irish bishops, and especially Cardinal Connell, responded vigorously according to

---

1. RTÉ, *Would you believe?*, 17 January 2011.
2. John Allen, 'Is Vatican letter on sex abuse a smoking gun?', *The Irish Catholic*, 27 January 2011.

Bishop Smith. One Irish Archbishop who could not be named in the *Would you believe?* programme for legal reasons, threatened to resign. This was because the Vatican was refusing to take action in a case which the DPP had declined to prosecute. In 1999 the Irish bishops met Cardinal Hoyos again on their five-yearly visit to Rome. At this meeting he again told them that the bishop's role was to be a father to his priests. In Michael Smith's view the Vatican did not see the issue as a crime, but rather as a moral issue between the priest and his bishop. They showed no awareness of its impact on the child or the wider society.

Within the Dublin diocese, according to Chapter 19 of the *Murphy Report*, the Chancellor of the diocese, Mgr Gerard Sheehy, opposed reporting cases to the police. This was because he regarded abuse as a symptom of disorder in the priest which needed treatment, not punishment.

The responses of the Vatican for a long time after the crisis emerged, as with the Irish bishops initially, were focused on a number of issues. The first was to protect the good name of the church and not scandalise the laity. The second was compassion for the priest. The third was to respect the 'father-son' relationship between the bishop and the priest. The fourth was clericalism: the issue was seen within the world view of pope, bishops and priests. Lay people were outside that circle, so they were less important.

Each of these is problematic. The scandal in the end was all the greater because of the way that church leaders responded. The compassion was in itself entirely appropriate: priests who abuse are human beings. They are loved by God whose love for them is not dependent on their actions. But, as Pope Benedict pointed out much later, compassion can be false if it overlooks the need for just punishment. In this case it overlooked the most critical element of the whole saga: the protection of children and the healing needed for those who had been abused and for their families. The 'father-son' relationship excluded the laity, which was also the problem with clericalism.

Indeed the exclusion of the laity illustrates how important theology is. Pre-Vatican II theology had emphasised the superiority of clerics within the church. Vatican II turned that upside down: all the members of the church were the 'People of God'.

Within that, different groups had particular roles but their primary church identity came from their baptism into the People of God. Unfortunately, that theology was not implemented after the council. The result was that a clerical model, instead of one based on the People of God, dominated.

The Pope's letter to the Catholics of Ireland

Part of Benedict XVI's response to the crisis was his letter to the Catholics of Ireland on 19 March 2010.[1] He starts by sharing in the 'the dismay and the sense of betrayal that so many of you have experienced on learning of these sinful and criminal acts and the way church authorities in Ireland dealt with them'. In his capacity as pastor of the universal church he had called the Irish bishops to Rome to give an account of their response to abuse in the past and to outline the steps they had taken for the future. His discussions with them and the senior officials of the Roman curia 'were frank and constructive'. He expressed his conviction 'that, in order to recover from this grievous wound, the church in Ireland must first acknowledge before the Lord and before others the serious sins committed against defenceless children'. He reminded Irish Catholics of the heroic contributions made to the church and to humanity as a whole by Irish people in the past, including great missionaries like Columbanus. Within Ireland, too, the church had endured persecution, including many martyrs like Oliver Plunkett. After Catholic Emancipation the church provided education, especially for the poor, and thereby made a great contribution to Irish society.

> In almost every family in Ireland, there has been someone – a son or a daughter, an aunt or an uncle – who has given his or her life to the church. Irish families rightly esteem and cherish their loved ones who have dedicated their lives to Christ, sharing the gift of faith with others, and putting that faith into action in loving service of God and neighbour.

However, in recent decades social change and secularisation has led to a decline in traditional devotion and priests and religious also adopted 'ways of thinking and assessing secular realities without sufficient reference to the gospel'. Vatican II was

1. *Pastoral Letter*, 19 March 2010.

sometimes misinterpreted. There was a well-intentioned but misguided tendency to avoid punishment when dealing with people through canon law. All of this is the overall context in which 'we must try to understand the disturbing problem of child sexual abuse'.

The Pope then lists a series of causes of the crisis: inadequate procedures for vetting candidates for the priesthood, poor formation in seminaries, clergy being put on a pedestal, a 'misplaced concern for the 'reputation of the church and the avoidance of scandal, resulting in failure to apply existing canonical penalties and to safeguard the dignity of every person'. He urged all the Catholics of Ireland to reflect on the wounds inflicted on Christ's body by the abuse.

To the victims he said:

You have suffered grievously and I am truly sorry. I know that nothing can undo the wrong you have endured. Your trust has been betrayed and your dignity has been violated. Many of you found that, when you were courageous enough to speak of what happened to you, no one would listen. Those of you who were abused in residential institutions must have felt that there was no escape from your sufferings. It is understandable that you find it hard to forgive or be reconciled with the church. In her name, I openly express the shame and remorse that we all feel. At the same time, I ask you not to lose hope. It is in the communion of the church that we encounter the person of Jesus Christ, who was himself a victim of injustice and sin. Like you, he still bears the wounds of his own unjust suffering. He understands the depths of your pain and its enduring effect upon your lives and your relationships, including your relationship with the church. I know some of you find it difficult even to enter the doors of a church after all that has occurred. Yet Christ's own wounds, transformed by his redemptive sufferings, are the very means by which the power of evil is broken and we are reborn to life and hope. I believe deeply in the healing power of his self-sacrificing love – even in the darkest and most hopeless situations – to bring liberation and the promise of a new beginning.

He called on priests and religious people who had abused children to take responsibility for what they had done and to repent. They had 'forfeited the esteem of the people of Ireland and brought shame and dishonour upon your confreres', but 'sincere repentance opens the door to God's forgiveness and the grace of true amendment.'

He offered his support to parents who had been shocked to learn of the abuse and encouraged young people, despite the changed context in which they are growing up, to seek Christ in the church.

He recognised the outrage and indignation that the abuse provoked, feelings shared by many priests and religious and he also acknowledged that many felt personally discouraged, 'even abandoned' and that in the eyes of some they were tainted by association.

He tells his brother bishops that some of them failed grievously which has seriously undermined their leadership and effectiveness. He calls on them and religious superiors to co-operate with the civil authorities 'in their area of competence'. 'Only decisive action carried out with complete honesty and transparency will restore the respect and good will of the Irish people towards the church to which we have consecrated our lives'. He calls on them to ensure that the laity are educated so that they can offer a convincing account of the gospel in the modern world.

In addressing all the faithful he says that 'measures to deal justly with individual crimes are essential' but he also calls for a new vision to inspire present and future generations to treasure the gift of our common faith.

At the end of the letter he called for some specific actions: penance on Fridays, making Lent a time to pray for God's mercy and strength, encouraging Eucharistic adoration, and holding a nationwide mission for bishops, priests and religious. As well as this he decided to conduct an Apostolic Visitation of some Irish dioceses, seminaries and congregations. This would be a listening exercise after which a report would be presented to Rome.

He recognised that great efforts had been made to ensure child safety in the church.

At the beginning of his letter Benedict said he was truly sorry. As we have seen, he admitted that the Vatican had been slow to respond. Many victims have stated that they want the Vatican to formally recognise its responsibility for the response to the abuse.

This letter addresses many of the key issues in the abuse crisis, but it neglects one central area: at no point does the Pope address the role of the Vatican.

The abuse crisis also shows the extent to which Irish bishops were deferential to the Vatican. Cardinal Hoyos was head of the Congregation for the Clergy. He was not the bishop of an Irish diocese. In the theology which focuses on the hierarchy of the church, the Pope and the bishops in union with him are the rulers of the church. Vatican departments are not superior in authority to bishops in their own dioceses. In canon law priests have a right to appeal to Rome beyond local tribunals. But the harm done to children by priests who abused them was so great that Irish bishops clearly should have acted collectively and with far greater vigour much earlier. A serious threat to resign, not by one archbishop, but by all the bishops of Ireland would surely have produced a faster Vatican response. The Ryan Report mentions deference as a key factor in the poor response to abuse. The Irish bishop's response to Rome is an example of this. Obviously the crimes should also have been reported to the police. The outcome was a disaster for those who were abused, and also for the church.

In the theology of Vatican II the church theoretically changed from a hierarchical model to one focused on the People of God. In this, lay people, religious, priests, bishops and Popes all have different roles, but all share a radical equality as baptised persons called to serve God and others. That vision was not followed after Vatican II and the hierarchical model continued to dominate. But does this mean that lay people are excluded from all responsibility for the response to abuse?

(c) Who was to Blame: Lay People?
The abuse and the response to it took place within a system. Bishops and religious superiors were part of that system, but so too were lay people. This will not be easy for many to hear.

Some lay people are guilty because they were directly involved in the institutions in which children were abused: workmen, cooks, cleaners, stationery, food and other types of suppliers, insurance and legal people, medical staff, police, judges, the Society for the Prevention of Cruelty to Children, journalists who sat on stories about abuse, parents who used Artane and other institutions as a threat when their children misbehaved, which means they knew something about the conditions – the list could go on. I am not saying that all those who were members of these groups were personally guilty. I am certain that many acted with great kindness and integrity and did the best they could within the circumstances prevailing, as also did many of the religious and priests who gave their lives to working in these institutions. But to the extent that individuals knew about abuse, did not oppose it, perhaps out of fear of losing their job, and continued their support for the work of institutions, to that extent they bear some personal guilt.

Secondly, some lay people, like clergy and religious, also bear personal responsibility in so far as they were part of, or contributed to, the culture that put clergy on a pedestal. The clergy could not have maintained their position without some lay collusion. Yes, clergy demanded this superior status and that was wrong. But it was also wrong that they were given the status.

> In any institution, including the church, it is not only those who are in leadership positions who maintain institutional cultures. For any culture to endure within an institution, a large proportion of the members of the institution have to support it, explicitly or implicitly, actively or passively. That a clericalist and conformist culture has survived within the church is a shared responsibility of us all.[1]

One obvious response to this is for lay people to say that it is not our church: 'It is the church of the bishops and the pope. *They* control all power in the church and keep it to themselves.' It is therefore a bit rich if, having responded disastrously to people who were abusing, and having excluded laity from decision making, they now want to involve us in responding to the crisis.' Some lay people therefore oppose the use of church collections for abuse payments.

---

1. Brendan Callaghan SJ, 'On scandal and scandals', in *Thinking Faith: the online journal of the British Jesuits,* 15 April 2010.

At first sight this seems a fair point. The church was controlled by bishops and religious superiors. But some lay people were personally guilty and they also contributed to the system of clericalism.

A friend of mine tells how when he was a young boy in a rural village in the 1950s he heard his parents talk about a local girl who was pregnant. She was fired from her job as a teacher and was sent away to England. The priests, the Gardaí, the teachers in the school, those local parents who knew about it, all colluded in this injustice. Most were upright, practicing Catholics. At the time they probably thought they were doing a good thing. Scandal had to be avoided. The small, closed community could not be contaminated and its good name had to be preserved. But no attention, in that context, was given to the rights and needs of the girl or her baby. Nor was there any focus on the father of the unborn child.

Many in 2010 look back at the terrible wrongs of the 1950s, and are rightly shocked. But they assume similar wrongs cannot happen in the modern world. Yet today people are confined in sub-human conditions in Mountjoy jail in Dublin and good Catholics seem unconcerned. In the US many otherwise good Christians support state execution. Many others are astonished at Muslims being angry at the US, despite the fact that hundreds of thousands have been killed by US arms. The point of this is not to use modern oblivion as a way to divert attention from the past, but rather, while condemning past wrongs to become aware also of our current blindness.

We can only be guilty of something if we have done wrong. Some lay people were personally guilty. But what about other lay people, or indeed other priests, religious and bishops who played no role in covering up wrong, who abused no one and indeed who never encountered anyone who did? Clearly these are not guilty of anything in this area. But as members of the church are they still connected to the abuse crisis in some way? This raises the question of corporate connectedness, and it is to that topic that we now turn.

(d) Corporate Connectedness?

We need to distinguish personal guilt from corporate connectedness. Each is important but different. Personal guilt is borne by individuals who did wrong. These include the priests and religious who carried out the abuse, bishops and superiors who knew about it and failed to respond appropriately, their superiors who either knew about the inadequate response and failed to deal with it or who actively blocked the bishops and superiors from responding, and lay people who contributed to the culture which made both the abuse and the response to it more likely.

Take the example of Germany after 1945. Under the Nazis over 6 million Jews, homosexuals, gypsies, people with special needs and others were butchered in the Holocaust. Clearly a large number of Germans were guilty. So were many in other countries: it is said that French trains for the concentration camps always left on time. But there were also many Germans who were not involved because they knew nothing about the Holocaust or because they actively opposed the Nazis. Dietrich Bonheoffer, the Lutheran minister, and Maximilian Kolbe, a Catholic priest who replaced a man picked out at random by the Nazis to be murdered, are examples. Further, Germans who were born after 1945 obviously were not guilty. Yet in the 1950s the German state started paying reparations to Israel. These funds came from taxes, and young Germans, like others, had to bear the cost.

Did the German state have a duty to do this, or was it a voluntary, charitable act?

A German born after 1945 might argue that none of her taxes should be used as reparation to the Jews because of her innocence, but she is also part of the new state and that raises questions about her corporate connectedness.

One view will argue that the German state is connected to the Jews. The state is the only mechanism that can represent the German people as a whole. It was the German people as a whole who are connected to the Holocaust.

A second view is that the state cannot be tied into the Holocaust for at least two reasons. First, the Nazi state was abolished in 1945. The Federal Republic of West Germany that eventually emerged was a new state. It therefore – in this view – did not inherit the Nazi state's liabilities. Second, it is not the German people as a whole but the individuals who participated in the Holocaust who are connected. They, and only they, should pay, because it is they and only they who are guilty.

Neither argument is entirely satisfactory. The Federal Republic was a new state. To make young Germans pay for the sins of some older Germans seems unfair. Yet the second argument is based on individualism. It takes no account of the myriad of ways in which people are linked. The Nazi regime was a system. Individuals, even if they opposed the state, were part of that system: if they worked, they paid taxes. They benefited from the state. If we accepted the individualistic approach it would mean that liability can only be attributed to individuals and this can only be done by way of individual prosecutions. There would be no communal mechanism to make reparations. That feels profoundly wrong. So, while there are difficulties in arguing that the new German state should take on the liability, there are greater difficulties in not doing so.

We could take other examples, such as the banking crisis of 2008, or the Northern Ireland conflict. Who was to blame for these? Were the people of Ireland, for example, who elected the politicians who oversaw the bankers, connected in any way to the financial crisis? In Northern Ireland in recent years there has been much focus on communal forgiveness. But this implies communal wrongdoing. So should the people of Ireland – or the nationalists in Ireland – apologise to the people of Britain for attacks by the IRA? Or should the people of Britain apologise for the Famine?

As you can see we could get into a major treatise on the issue because corporate connectedness is complex. My suspicion is that there are cases where the concept applies and others where it does not. The question raised by it is: 'Are you connected in some way to the abuse crisis?' The instinctive answer of most people is: 'I'm not guilty.'

In fact this is not an answer to the question because the question asked is about being connected, the answer given is about guilt. Like young Germans born after World War II one can be connected without being guilty. Nonetheless it is difficult for us to separate the notions of connectedness and guilt. Most of us want no connection with terrible events such as the Holocaust, or clerical child abuse. So the questions arise: Apart from those who were personally guilty, who else was involved? In what way? With what responsibilities?

(i) Is the church corporately connected?

The church is not a state. It is not even one legal entity: each diocese and religious congregation is separate. In church law no bishop in Ireland is accountable to any other bishop. No bishop is accountable to the Cardinal. No bishop is accountable to the Irish Bishops' Conference. The only person a bishop is accountable to is the pope.

If you do a building job for the Dominicans and they don't pay you and you come looking to us Jesuits for the money you won't get it.

This suggests that the way to deal with claims for abuse is through individual congregations and dioceses. But if you take that line, why not go further? The congregation as a whole did no wrong: it was the individual who abused, or the particular superior who responded inadequately who did wrong. Let the individual, not the congregation, pay.

The argument does not stand up because many religious congregations take on the duty of meeting the financial liabilities of their members. The organisation thereby becomes liable for their members. In the case of diocesan priests, the diocese is involved because in many cases the priest concerned was acting on behalf of the diocese, and/or using his role as a priest, when committing the crime.

Further, in the case of abuse, both the wrong committed against children and the damage done to the church's call to be a sign of the presence of God is so great that it is entirely reasonable to expect dioceses and religious orders, even if not immediately involved, to take on some of the response that is needed.

(ii) Does corporate connectedness include lay people?

Lay people are members of the church. Church law does not treat them as full members, but that does not change the theological reality, spelt out in Vatican II among other sources, that they are full members. Lay people define themselves as Catholic. For some this can mean that they are connected to God through Christ and may even take part in the sacraments, but at the same time they do not see themselves as connected to the institution. They see the institution as clerical and they want nothing to do with it. The abuse crisis is one major factor in developing this attitude. But the church is also an institution, however flawed. Other lay people see themselves as members of the institution. To the extent that they do, they are connected with the abuse crisis. It is our church that institutionally was guilty of the terrible response to the abuse. If we are members then we are connected. In this respect the position of innocent lay people and clerics is no different. Their connection to the crisis is not necessarily because they are guilty but because they are members of the church.

How are we connected? In several ways. One is through shame: we feel shame at what our church has done as an institution. In this respect our response is similar to parents who feel ashamed at what one of their children has done, even though the parents are entirely innocent. Secondly, we face being blamed by people who are not church members. This is something clergy and religious face more than lay people, although there is no difference between the two unless personal guilt is involved. Thirdly, we face some financial consequences: the funds of the institution, to which we contributed, will be used to make recompense. Fourthly, we face a challenge as members: how do we change the institution so that the response that took place to the abuse can never happen again?

One of the key causes of the abuse crisis was that we maintained a clerical church which marginalised lay people in direct opposition to the focus of Vatican II on the People of God. If this is to change, all of us, clerical and lay, have a corporate duty to bring that change about. We will not break clerical control of the church without vehement and committed lay involvement. It is quite right that church funds are paid to those who were abused. But these funds have been contributed by lay people. Lay people have, therefore, both a duty and a right to play a role in decisions about the spending of these funds. The new theological model so desperately needed in the church will not emerge without lay involvement. A better approach, then, is not to oppose the use of church collections for abuse payments since these are part of the church's corporate response to the crisis, but instead to ensure that in future clergy will never have control of finances without lay oversight.

In the past and the present, the marginalisation of lay people in the church was and is a major problem for the church. Do we want to change this? If so, it means that lay people have to take on a role of corporate responsibility in the church even before the law of the church or the theology of its leaders in theory makes this possible.

After the Ryan and Murphy reports it was very tempting simply to ignore the institutional church. So many efforts have been made to reform it since Vatican II. Despite this, clericalism and lay marginalisation seem nearly as strong today as ever. Yet to the extent that we ignore the institution while remaining members of it, to that extent we face the charge of colluding in maintaining structures that because they lack adequate account-ability contributed to the abuse crisis. Only if we actively campaign for change in the church, however difficult that may be, can we avoid this charge of collusion.

Insufficient attention has been paid to the issue of corporate connectedness in the abuse crisis and its implications. Discussing and probing the issue can help up us not only to understand the past but to avoid similar disasters in the future.

To sum up this section: we distinguished between personal guilt and corporate connectedness. At a personal level the following bear guilt because of the abuse:

- those who carried it out.
- those who knew the addictive nature of abuse and still failed to respond adequately when they knew those in their authority had abused.
- those higher up in authority in the church who knew about inadequate local responses and either did nothing about this or actively blocked local superiors when the latter wanted to act.
- lay people who contributed services in support of the system while knowing about the abuse and did nothing about it.
- those of the wider membership of the church who contributed to a culture in which there was encouragement for patriarchy, lack of accountability and deference to the clergy, all of which made the failure to respond adequately more likely.

At a corporate level, all the current members of the church, al-though most are personally innocent, are connected because of the failure of our church to respond adequately to the crisis. We therefore bear a responsibility to work for change in the church.

The church is meant to be a sign of the presence of God in the world. In part that involves protecting and cherishing children. The response to the abuse crisis was the direct opposite of this.

This has made belief in God more difficult for many and being a Catholic makes no sense without this belief. So in the next section I want to turn to two questions: How can I believe in God?, and Who is God?

SECTION TWO

Who Is God?

CHAPTER THREE

Believe in God, or Not?

Belief in God is about a choice. In that respect it is similar to any other relationship.

That probably is not how we usually think of relationships. We meet someone. We find ourselves spending time with them. At first there does not seem to be much choice in this: we just happen to be where the other is. Yet in practice we are choosing the whole time: how we smile or glare, how our face lights up or not, how close we allow ourselves to get physically, whether or not we agree to meet the other outside of work, or whatever.

There is often a lot of denial at the start of a relationship: 'He's no different from anyone else'; 'He's just a friend'; 'He's good fun'. There is a good reason for this: relationships are threatening because if we allow ourselves to care deeply for someone we can get hurt badly.

Gradually, however, we notice the other is in our minds more often. Funny things start happening to our bellies. Our ears prick up when we hear his or her name mentioned. A ringing phone takes on a new significance. (It can be quite amusing to hear the almost audible disappointment – almost immediately covered up of course – when I phone a family and a teenager answers: apparently I am not the 'he' that she was waiting for!)

In the end we choose. We become an 'item'. We introduce our partner to friends and family. We go public. Eventually many will marry, but of course there are other options such as life-long friendships.

It is important to stress the role of choice in all this because choice is related to commitment. That is not a popular word with many. Does it mean that I have to stay with her when I no longer love her? Or when she is no longer helping my self-fulfilment? If this is the case then I might end up unfulfilled, and that surely is unthinkable.

Yes, actually, commitment does mean facing the possibility of unfullfillment. It means closing off other doors. It means ruling out some other relationships. It is about going through a narrow door, with no guarantees. That is what 'in sickness and in health' in the marriage ceremony is about. And there will be many times in every marriage when each partner will have to choose to go on with it, and to do so in unattractive circumstances. Yet each of these choices may open up new and unforeseeable horizons. That is what commitment is about: when faced with the blank door, we stick it out, we look for ways through the door when none seems possible, to search for new depths in ourselves and in the other. (This is not to suggest that partners should always stay together: there are times, for example in cases of domestic violence, that an abused partner should certainly leave.) Relating to God has some similarities but also many differences.

Many of us are introduced to God as children. We are taught to pray at bed time and asked whom we want to pray for. That in part is why angels are becoming so popular. In a world where many are rejecting church-based religion, angels can be a reminder of the comforts and certainties of childhood. In the old days many families said the rosary. As we go through school we may simply lose touch with faith. We start questioning. We may find proofs for God's existence unconvincing. Our friends give up going to Mass, so it becomes cool to follow them. Besides, Mass is boring. So we drop out.

We may still have faith. We go to funeral Masses, not only to support our friends, but also because we want to pray for the dead person. We turn to God, sometimes desperately, in the middle of exams, or when threatened with loss in a relationship. This is the 'one-armed bandit' God: he (and it is usually a male God) is like a slot machine. If we put in enough prayers or novenas at the right time maybe we will get lucky and get a pay out. I hope this God does not exist.

Sometimes people go through a second religious phase when they have their own children. It happens naturally because they start teaching the children to pray – since this is what their parents did to them, and despite the fervent desire of many not to imitate their parents that is precisely what they do. Some of this is about hoping for a life beyond death for their child. Some of it may be out of fear of God. Or it can be about rediscovering aspects of faith from earlier in life that were important at the time, and which now seem important again.

Others, of course, find that faith means a lot to them. In fact it becomes the most important thing in their lives.

For all of us, choosing affects our faith. Some choose to ignore it. So they have a vague sense that there is something 'up there', probably with a beard on it. But it does not interfere too much with life. Life is too short. There are many questions we can't answer, so it is better to leave it all alone. When death comes, well that is just one more of these unanswerable questions.

Others are more critical. They look at the evidence, find the God arguments wanting and choose atheism. Some of these see religious people as simply failing to grow up and face the world the way it is: we are part of evolution. When we die we get recycled as grass, or whatever. Not facing up to this is about fear in the face of unanswerable questions.

Believing in God is made particularly difficult by evil. Those who suffered abuse from representatives of the church must surely know this more than most.

The older I get I often feel attracted by the secularist arguments: when we die the brain stops, disintegrates and in 5-10 years there is only an empty skull. Whatever is left is not a human person. Believing in God means believing that there is more, that I do not stop existing, that the 'I' in me continues beyond the disintegration of the body.

I want to believe. But wanting it proves nothing. Projection, need fulfilment, fear of nothingness, a failure to face up to the recycling of everything in creation – these are the charges that rise up in response to my wanting.

Yet tonight before I sleep I will pray. And I will believe that this is important. Important to me, but also important to God. Maybe I will feel the presence of God, maybe I won't. But I will still believe it important. If I miss the prayer for a while, then I will literally miss it. I will know things are not right. I will want to come back to it, however difficult it is.

Tomorrow morning I may hear the sound of my own feet as I walk up and down in my flat. I may hear a silence. In that silence I may hear God. When I do hear God I no longer have doubts, but certainty. Of course the certainty is subject to all the secularist challenges. But when the silence is there the arguments against faith make no impact on me. One moment of that experience is enough to draw me towards God, to want to know God more, to reject all other possibilities, to want to see the world and other people as God sees them.

There are other reasons. The most important of these by far is my relationships. Knowing somebody well makes his or her death somehow ridiculous. He or she cannot really be dead. That is denial – part of coming to terms with bereavement. But it can also be an affirmation that the inner core of the person is not dead: he or she is too alive to die.

It is also something else: it is a belief that the other person, although one with his or her body, is more than this. Relationships move from the outside to the inside: from the lustful look to the encounter with the person when the body is no longer noticed, except as a matter of concern or joy. We know each other through our bodies but our knowing goes way beyond them.

In a certain sense I believe because I choose to believe. I do not do it because the evidence is overwhelming. But in another sense I do not choose. I am chosen. I am gifted. And there are parallels between this and our relationships.

Sometimes when a relationship goes wrong we can learn how much it really matters to us. That may be because we are faced with new decisions. But it can also be because we are suddenly faced with the prospect of life without the other. If the relationship is going through a bad time, living without the other may be attractive for a time. 'I don't need this nonsense. She or he is crazy and is always going to be crazy. He or she should get help instead of driving me mad. Wouldn't it be great if I was with someone else, someone normal, someone who could make me laugh, or feel good, or lift me instead of depressing me in this relationship? Freedom beckons, big time: anything is better than being trapped.

Yet at the same time as these thoughts and feelings are swirling around there may be a different feeling. Probably one with fewer words, but one that is deeper. And it is deeper because it matters more. The deeper desire is to be with the other. Not only is that desire deeper but we can become aware of the horror of what life would really be like without him or her; a horror at losing all that you have shared together; of the connectedness between you, of the immediacy of understanding, the caring, the commitment. And when we are in touch with that desire – and it may take a long time to get there – then we know what we want: we want the relationship to go forward into something new, not what it was in the past, but something that takes account of the past and moves forward.

In the middle of this experience we sometimes realise that our own choosing may be quite small in all this. This does not make it unimportant. But when we are in touch with our deepest desires there can be a sense that we did not choose them. In some way they were given to us; they are a gift.

I have often wondered about my own relationship with God, even about my own decision to become a Jesuit. Yes, I did choose in the sense that I got into the car so that my parents could drive me to the noviceship, after years of trying to avoid this. And I felt a lot of apprehension, even dread, as I did that, but I still went ahead. So, yes, I did choose. But there was always a sense that I was being pulled towards something, drawn in, and that however much I would resist, the pull would still be there.

It's still that way in my prayer.

Believing in God is perhaps a crazy statement that people are more than the physical, that what matters most is between the brain cells, not the cells themselves. It is a denial that the grave is the final statement about life, an affirmation that we go beyond the grave.

In our liturgy we pray that the soul may be at rest as we wait for the resurrection on the Last Day. The theologians tell us that there is no time in the next life, but I find small comfort in that. When I die I do not want to wait until some rock smashes this earth to pieces, or till the philosophers and scientists work out that there cannot be an end to life. No, I want to see those I have loved immediately – whatever about there being no time in eternity.

If the next life is anything like this, and if there is one, and if we are still the persons we are today, then we will not stop growing. Rather we will finally realise that we are destined to grow for all eternity.

In the end I do believe. I believe that I will see God face to face. I am certain that I will be filled with crushing disappointment that I failed so often to live my life to the full. But I will also see a face of mystery and wonder looking at me and seeing many things in me that I know not of.

I will also see a face consumed with love for all of the people who have lived. Then I will know at last that I can only know God with and through others. And eternity will be about exploring what that means.

I can, then, believe in God, even if this belief is also challenged. That was one of the tests I had to face in answering the question, can I stay in the Catholic Church? For the Christian, however, it is not enough to explore our personal search for God alone. We do it as part of a community and a community with a history. That history begins with the Bible, first in the Old Testament, that series of texts that we share in common with Our Lord's own people the Jews. It is to this Old Testament that I now want to turn to discover what nuggets it contains to answer the question: Who is God?

CHAPTER FOUR

Who is the Christian God?

The Christian is a person, an individual. As such he or she has to struggle with doubts and questions. Many older people complain that faith, religion and the church are not the same now as they were when they were children. Nor should they be. They are no longer children. They live in a world of questions with great emphasis given to reason. That emphasis has led to improvements in our lives, for example in medicine. But it has also raised doubts about many religious beliefs. These doubts have developed further as scholars have brought scientific methods to bear on the scriptures.

What do the scriptures tell us about God? It is worth picking out a few themes first from the Old and then from the New Testament. These will not answer all our questions, or take away all our doubts but they may remind us of some of the things we already know about God's love, compassion, anger at sin and forgiveness.

THEMES FROM THE OLD TESTAMENT

Friendship with God
People often tell me that they have problems relating to the Old Testament. Some of this is due to readings they hear at Mass which are sometimes about the Israelites cutting the heads off their enemies, or sometimes getting the same treatment themselves.

Violence is certainly part of the Old Testament story, but there is a lot more in it. One great character is Moses. As with all the great characters in the Bible his birth is special: the Egyptian ruler the Pharaoh decides that the Israelites are getting too numerous so he orders all Jewish males to be killed at birth. But he did not reckon with Moses' mother. She sent her daughter out with the baby placed in a papyrus basket and told her to leave it near the Nile. Pharaoh's daughter comes to the river to bathe and hears the baby crying. She sends one of her servants to fetch it and feels sorry for the baby when she sees it. Then Moses' sister appears and offers to fetch a Hebrew woman to nurse the child for Pharaoh's daughter who agrees to this. Being a resourceful child she brings her own mother who then not only gets her baby back but ensures that in seven years time she will be able to bring him back to Pharaoh's daughter and get him a good education and position in the Egyptian palace.

If Moses turned out to be bright, and he did, it is not surprising considering the intelligence shown in appalling circumstances by his mother and sister.

He must always have felt an outsider. A Jew, he was reared for much of his life in the Egyptian court and benefited from this. But he had to flee when he killed an Egyptian overseer who was beating one of his workers. While fleeing he helped a group of women to get water when they were being harassed by shepherds. Their father, Reuel, was so grateful that he gave Moses his daughter Zipporah in marriage. He named his first son Gershom because, he said, 'I am an alien in a foreign land' (Ex 2:22).

His first encounter with God was when he was looking after his father-in-law's sheep. He saw a flame blazing in the middle of a burning bush, but the bush was not being burnt up. When he went closer to investigate he heard a voice telling him to take off his shoes because the ground he was walking on was holy. A voice from the bush said: 'I am the God of your ancestors, the God of Abraham, the God of Isaac and the God of Jacob. At this Moses covered his face, for he was afraid to look at God' (Ex 3: 6).

The Burning Bush was adopted by some of the Reformers at the time of the Reformation and it is the official symbol of the Presbyterian Church in Ireland. It is a symbol of the transcendence of God: Moses takes off his shoes. He covers his face. It is also a symbol of God's mysteriousness: a burning fire not only gives heat, but people often spend time just gazing into a fire: like water it seems to touch something basic in us.

That awe of the transcendent God stayed with Moses all his life, but we soon see other aspects of their relationship.

God calls Moses to lead his people to freedom, but Moses is reluctant. He has no qualifications. In fact he has several apparent disqualifications. God wants him to go to Pharaoh to demand freedom for the Jews, but Moses is fleeing from Pharaoh. Secondly, Moses is a bad speaker. Presumably he spoke with a foreign accent, having spent so long at the Egyptian court. But he also seems to have had a stammer. Yahweh gently points out that it is Yahweh who makes people dumb or gives them ability to speak. But Moses is persistent – a quality he will need later in dealing with Yahweh – and asks him to choose anyone in the whole world other than himself. Yahweh gets angry with him but eventually they reach a compromise: Moses' brother, Aaron can do the public speaking, but at the direction of Moses. So, in the end, Moses accepts the job God has given him and sets off for Egypt.

What happens next is shocking: we are told, 'God tried to kill Moses in the middle of the night. Zipporah, his wife, circumcised her son and touched Moses with the foreskin, saying: 'You are my blood-bridegroom (Ex 4:26)'. So Yahweh let him go. Weird stuff. But we get nowhere in understanding the Bible unless we are willing to tackle difficult as well as attractive texts. Steve Rodeheaver gives an insightful reflection on the text, which is worth reading in full.[1]

Rodeheaver suggests that the attempted killing by Yahweh is a symbol of the real death to which God calls all of us: the death to our own selfishness and our refusal to surrender to God. The attempted killing is a symbol. It seems that at this point Moses had not been circumcised so Zipporah's action was a symbolic circumcision of him. Circumcision became an identity symbol for the Israelites. It was a sign of the covenant or agreement that God made with Abraham and with the whole people and marked them as belonging to God (although the patriarchal limits of the symbol are striking). 'It is a sign of costly grace … Circumcision is more than just the surgical procedure of removing a piece of skin. It involves bearing the mark of God upon one's heart, yielding ownership of the heart to God, surrendering the centre of one's being to God'. The Israelites are told to 'Circumcise therefore the foreskin of your heart' (Deut 10:16). In the New Testament baptism replaces circumcision and is seen as a dying with Christ in order to rise with him. 'It is only via this death that one can receive the newness of life offered in Christ.'

---

1. Steve Rodeheaver, *Exodus 4:18-31: God Seeks Moses' Life*, © CRI/Voice, Institute, 2010.

Moses clearly went through that purifying process because his relationship with God deepened. We see him constantly struggling with God's anger. Indeed in many of the stories it seems as if he is the good guy and God the bad guy. This is because the scriptural writers like ourselves are gradually understanding some aspects of God, but not others (like ourselves). The part that they get hold of is God's anger at the disloyalty of the people. This is not about a religion separated from life. Throughout the story of Moses the covenant or agreement with God is mentioned constantly. God will be the people's God and the people will be God's people. But this is not automatic. People expel themselves from the covenant community by their actions, by failing to worship God, by not keeping the law, above all by not treating with respect widows, orphans, foreigners and other marginalised groups. That incurs the anger of God, and this is because God is a passionate lover. Look at how we react when one of our loved ones is hurt wrongly. If this is our reaction, God, who loves infinitely more than we do, is going to react infinitely stronger.

What is remarkable, however, about Moses is that in his relationship with God he moves to a stage of great intimacy. We are told that Moses set up a special tent outside the camp which was called the tent of meeting. The people would go out to the tent whenever they wanted to consult Yahweh. However, whenever Moses himself went out to it all the people would stand up and the men would stand at the door of their tents and watch him until he went into it. Then the pillar of cloud, which was the symbol of the presence of Yahweh that had led the people out of slavery in Egypt, would come down and station itself at the door of the tent. The people would then bow low. But, we are told, 'Yahweh would talk to Moses face to face, as a man talks to his friend' (Ex 33:11).

What an amazing picture for a Jewish writer to present of the relationship between God and a human being! Before this we have the transcendence of God emphasised: Moses taking off his shoes when he sees the Burning Bush; the clouds, thunder and lightening on Mount Sinai when Moses goes up the mountain to be with God. But here we see almost a friendship of equals, certainly of respect and intimacy. It is remarkable that so early in their history the Jewish people were able to conceive of such a relationship alongside one of awe and transcendence.

Western society is perhaps more focused on relationships of equals than ones of awe. It is not that intimacy and awe are opposed to each other. There should be an element of awe in our closest relationships, even if we might be slow to admit it to our loved ones! But it is surely surprising for Jewish people who, like surrounding groups, would have had a view of God which emphasised fear, transcendence and otherness in their dealings with God to see Moses' relationship with Yahweh as one of great intimacy.

Three other themes from the Old Testament should be mentioned. One is compassion.

Compassion
Over and over again we are told in the Old Testament that God is compassionate. It seems surprising given what we have seen of the emphasis on God's anger. Yet because the source of that anger was passionate love it is not actually surprising. People have their own favourite passages showing this intimacy. Popular examples are:

- Isaiah 43:1-4: we are reminded that it was Yahweh who created us, who formed us in the womb and who has redeemed us. So 'Do not be afraid'. Yahweh has called us by name. (As Mary Magdalene, 'the apostle of the apostles', will be called by name in the garden after the resurrection, Jn 20:16). 'You are mine.' No matter what happens to us Yahweh will be with us: 'Should you walk through fire, you will not suffer.' Yahweh has given up whole nations for us because `You are priceless to me. I love you and honour you'. This sounds crazy: Yahweh is honouring us. Yet that is what the text says.
- Going back to the story of Moses we hear Yahweh saying to him: 'And the Lord passed by before him, and proclaimed, "the Lord, the Lord God, merciful and gracious, long suffering, and abundant in goodness and truth, keeping mercy for thousands, forgiving iniquity and transgression and sin ..."' (Exodus 34:5-7). This is a

different picture from that of the angry God which many people find in the Old Testament.

- Hosea 11:1-4: An image used in the book is that Israel – the people – is like an unfaithful wife whom God constantly forgives. A second image is of Israel as a child: 'When Israel was a child, I loved him, and I called my son out of Egypt ... I myself taught Ephraim how to walk, I myself took them by the arm, but they did not know I was caring for them, with leading-strings of love, that, with them, I was like someone lifting an infant to his cheek and that bent down to feed him.'

Yes, the Israelites knew about the anger of God and they feared God. But they also knew about God's passionate and never-ending compassion for them.

Justice

Another theme woven into the Old Testament is justice. The prophets rail against people who abuse it. Amos is a good example. His book was written probably between 760 and 753 years before Christ was born, which makes it nearly 3000 years old. Is it relevant today?

They hate the man who teaches justice at the city gate
and detest anyone who declares the truth.
For trampling on the poor
and for extorting levies on their wheat;
although you have built houses of dressed stone,
you will not live in them;
although you have planted pleasant vineyards,
you will not drink wine from them:
for I know how many your crimes are
and how outrageous your sins,
you oppressors of the upright,
who hold people to ransom
and thrust the poor aside at the gates.
That is why anyone prudent
keeps silent now,
since the time is evil (Amos 5:10-13).

Yahweh is a passionate lover and passionate lovers are angry when their loved ones are hurt. We have seen a lot of injustice in Ireland, both in Northern Ireland and the Republic, in the past forty years. That injustice has made God angry. It matters to God when people are murdered in conflict or drug wars, when some make vast sums of money and schools are left without adequate toilets, or when the elderly or children are abused. It seems to matter particularly to God when these things are done by people who claim to be loving God:

> I hate, I scorn your festivals,
> I take no pleasure in your solemn assemblies.
> When you bring me your burnt offerings, your oblations,
> I do not accept them
> and I do not look at your communion sacrifices of fat cattle.
> Spare me the din of your chanting,
> Let me hear none of your strumming on lyres,
> but let justice flow like water,
> and uprightness like a never-failing stream! (Amos 5:21-24).

Does this seem vaguely familiar? Is Amos simply talking about his own time, or do similar things happen in our own? If so, it does not matter who we are – priest, prophet or king – we are all subject to the judgement of God. That judgement is made by a compassionate lover, but precisely because this is so God is also deeply angry, especially when we oppress others and pretend to love God.

God's forgiveness

Finally, the God who is a lover and who is also angry at wrongdoing, is also one who forgives. Time and again we are told that the people do wrong. Time and again God forgives them. 'Though your sins are like scarlet, they shall be as white as snow; though they are red as crimson, they shall be like wool' (Is 1:18).

Even King David, that great friend of God, who committed the appalling crime of taking Bathsheba, wife of Uriah, for his own sexual pleasure and ordering his military commander Joab to send Uriah into the thickest part of the battle so that he would certainly be killed, even he is forgiven (2 Sam 11:5-27).

No matter how bad the people have acted the passionate love of God is still available to them. All they need to do is to turn away from their sins and repent. That means confessing what they have done wrong, admitting their guilt, addressing issues of restitution (and the Jews had many laws about this), accepting just punishment and making a firm purpose of amendment.

Conclusion

This brief look at a few themes in the Old Testament shows us that the Jewish people developed an image of God as a passionate lover and close personal friend, someone that Moses could talk to as a man talks to his friend. But that deep love is also the reason why God is so angry when God's people are hurt wrongly: justice matters enormously to God. At the same time God is always ready to forgive when the people turn away from wrongdoing, and repent. The God of the Old Testament is much more attractive than many realise.

It is also worth noting that the people were very important in the Old Testament. In Israelite society people bound themselves to others in covenants. These were mostly social commitments, such as marriage, treaties, etc. This is true also of God's covenants. They were made with Abraham, Isaac, Jacob and other leaders, but they were made also with the whole people and their descendants. Through the covenant they were the Chosen People. That covenant continues today, but there is also a new covenant for us, the younger brothers and sisters of Jesus' own people. By that covenant we are called to follow Christ.

Having looked at some themes in the Old Testament, the book we share with Christ's own people the Jews, what does the New Testament tell us about who God is?

Christians believe that Jesus Christ is the revelation of God. He is the second person of the Blessed Trinity. He is fully human and fully divine. For Christians, the answer to the question 'How do we learn about God?' is to look at Christ.

What themes do we see in Christ's life? What sort of things did he emphasise? In this section we look at diversity, respect, patriarchy, superiority, deference, transparency and account-ability. As we shall see later all these themes will be important when we come to look at church structures, and are arguably directly related to the response to the clerical abuse scandal.

Diversity

Many people have remarked that Jesus' relations with women were strikingly different from the patriarchal culture in which he lived. One example, not without its problems, is his encounter with the Canaanite woman (Mt 15:21-28).

The woman's daughter is possessed. She is desperate to find a cure. She hears that Jesus is coming and rushes out to meet him. She begs for help. Jesus does not answer her at all. But this woman was persistent (something that Jesus often praised), so much so that his disciples finally went to him and begged him to see her because she was driving them crazy with her screaming. Desperate people can be like that: they keep on screaming.

Jesus again refuses and for a reason: he was sent only to the lost house of Israel. He is Jewish. The Chosen People are Jewish. It is to them that he has been sent. This woman is not Jewish. So he should not respond to her.

Then the woman came and knelt before him: she humbled herself and again begged: 'Lord, help me'. It was the sort of utterly transparent prayer to which Jesus responds on many other occasions. But again he argues that he is sent only to the Chosen People and he does it in a way that seems insulting and arrog-ant: 'It is not fair to take the children's bread and throw it to the dogs.' Even this is not enough to put off the woman. She re-sponds: 'Yes, Lord, yet even the dogs eat the crumbs that fall from their master's table.'

At this Jesus exclaims at the depth of her faith and her daughter was healed instantly.

The story is an uncomfortable one. It does not fit with the image of 'Jesus, meek and mild', and that is not surprising since it is quite clear that neither of these describes Jesus well. This is not a story of a welcoming, compassionate or understanding Jesus, but rather of someone living within ethnic boundaries. Why then is the story one of my favourites?

Because it shows Jesus learning. The idea that Jesus had something to learn, or actually learnt, is a surprise to many. It should not be. The story of the Incarnation is one of God becoming human, not superhuman; of God entering into our world; of God becoming like us in all things except sin. To be human is to learn. The day we stop learning we die.

In the story Jesus, a Jew, encounters a woman who was not of his group. He was focused on his mission, a mission to his own people. She did not fit into this category. There was nothing particularly surprising about Jesus' attitude: he was a Jew of his time. That is what the incarnation means. But what matters most in this story is not his initial reaction to the woman, nor even her persistent pleading, but the fact that eventually he responds to her. He responds eventually because he has learnt something: that God's message goes beyond his own Jewish people. He learnt this because, in the end, he listened to the woman. She was his teacher.

For a Jewish man to learn from a foreigner was significant. It was a recognition that there was more to the world than his own Jewish world. For a Jewish man to learn from a woman was even more striking: men were seen as being superior to women in that culture. Jesus was recognising an equality between him and the woman. He allowed his own cultural limitations to be challenged by a foreign woman. He grew as a person because of her challenge.

Some people interpret this story differently. They point out that Jesus was one with God. So he could not have learnt because learning implies there are things that he does not know. Therefore in the story he really knew what he was going to do and the dialogue with the woman was designed to test her faith.

This argument is incorrect on several counts. First, it fails to take the incarnation seriously. Jesus, the second person of the Trinity really became human. To be human is not to know everything. Learning and discovery is at the centre of what it is to be human from the first time a baby begins to hear, to feel and to see. Jesus, like the rest of us, had to learn. Secondly, as a human he was part of a particular group and culture, with all the limits and the richness that implies. He could only learn about the richness of other cultures, and be challenged in his natural Jewish-centred view of the world by encountering people from cultures different from his own. Thirdly, the story shows Jesus being startled at the faith of the woman. This happens in several other encounters that Jesus had with foreigners, for example the centurion who came to him asking that he cure his servant. Finally, the text says nothing about Jesus testing the faith of the woman. It shows him responding negatively to her at first, and only gradually changing through his encounter with her until he treated her as an equal.

The story is striking because Jesus learnt how not to be arrogant. He learnt the importance and richness of people from different cultures. He learnt a lesson that the early church would struggle with, as we shall see in the disputes between Paul and the other disciples over receiving the Gentiles, who were not Jews, into what was at first an all-Jewish church.

That focus on diversity was also seen in the way he allowed sinners to touch him. When he was at a meal with Simon, one of the Pharisees, a woman came in suddenly, knelt behind him, started weeping and wiped his feet with her tears and with ointment. The Pharisees, being good living, were scandalised that he did not keep himself separate from a sinner. But Jesus told a parable about one man owing someone a large sum of money and one owing a little. Both were forgiven. Which of the two men, Jesus asked, would have greater love for the man who forgave them? 'The one who was let off more, I suppose', Simon answered. Jesus then pointed out how Simon had not poured any water over his feet when he arrived, had given him no kiss, had not anointed his head with oil. But the woman had done all these things. And then he turned and spoke to the woman with a message that was shocking to the Pharisees but good news for her: 'Your sins are forgiven.' It was shocking to the Pharisees because only God can forgive sins. How could Jesus, a mere man like the rest of them, know that God had forgiven her? (Lk 7:36-50).

That struggle for diversity, for acceptance of difference, for recognition of the marginalised, is still present in our church today.

Respect

Respect was a big value for the Jesus that we see in the gospels. Yet it was often respect with confrontation.

One of the major conflicts is between Jesus and the Pharisees. Some of this undoubtedly reflects divisions between the early followers of Christ, who were all Jews, and their fellow Jews who did not see him in the same light as they did. However, it would be surprising if some of it does not go back to the historical Jesus. What was the conflict about?

There were various issues. One was the pomp and ceremony of the Pharisees. Jesus condemned 'the hypocrites' who liked to let people know they were praying and fasting. 'They have had their reward' (Mt 6:2). He told his followers not to be like those who love to let the whole world know when they give alms so as to win people's admiration. (Alms were even more important in that society because there was no social welfare, just as there is none today in many countries).

Then the hypocrites love to say their prayers standing up in the synagogue and at the street corners so that everyone will see them. Jesus told the story of the Pharisee and the tax collector who went up to the Temple to pray. The Pharisee said: 'I thank you, God, that I am not grasping, unjust, adulterous, like everyone else, particularly that I am not like this tax collector here. I fast twice a week. I pay tithes on all I get' (Lk 18:9-14). The tax collector simply prayed for mercy because he was a sinner.

This was a shocking story to Jesus' listeners. They would have agreed with the tax collector: the tax collector was a sinner, and a bad one. In fact he was so bad that most of the people hated him. He colluded with the Roman occupiers who polluted the holy places. He and his colleagues oppressed the people by grinding the last shekel they could get out of them in taxes and then paid off their Roman masters. Yes, they would definitely have agreed that he was a sinner. They almost certainly would not have liked the conclusion of Jesus' story: the tax collector went down to his house at rights with God.

Yet Jesus was showing something profound in the story: he was teaching that no matter who a person is he or she is worthy of respect simply because he or she is a person. The Pharisee was no better than the tax collector. In fact he was worse because he depended on himself, not on God. The tax collector, who was a sinner, recognised that he was a sinner and asked for forgiveness. Jesus respected all people, no matter who they were.

Another example of him being unimpressed by apparent human greatness was when he saw the widow putting the mite into the Temple collection. It was a tiny amount. But it was all she had. Jesus focused on that, not on the great amounts given in public by the rich.

Jesus emphasised real values, not legal gymnastics to get around laws. So he challenged different Jewish laws. On divorce he said anyone who divorces his wife, except in the case of an illicit marriage, makes her an adulteress; and anyone who marries a divorced woman commits adultery. This raises a complex discussion about divorce, marital breakdown and remarriage. But the reason for referring to the story here is to notice the way that Jesus focuses on respect: the society, as we have noted, was a patriarchal one. Men had the power to dismiss their wives. That left the wives powerless and marginalised. No other man would be likely to take her on. Her economic prospects were extremely limited. So a major purpose of Jesus' teaching on divorce, in that society, was to see that women were treated with respect.

He condemned those who saw the splinter in their brother's or sister's eye and could not see the plank in their own.

He lacerated the Pharisees and others who kept many customs about ceremonial washing before meals and who observed other human traditions, but not God's law of love. He exposed their hypocrisy when they turned to their parents and said all their property was 'Korban' or dedicated to God, so that they did not have to care for their aged parents (Mk 7:11-12).

He was unimpressed by their laws of ritual cleanliness: 'Nothing that goes into someone from the outside can make that person unclean; it is the things that come out of someone that makes that person unclean' (Mk 7:15).

Respect for persons was at the centre of his teaching. It was not external show, pomp and ceremony, or external religious practice that mattered, but treating people with respect and justice.

A male-dominated society

The culture in which Jesus lived was certainly influenced by patriarchy.

The Holiness Code (Lev 17-26) is an example: it is a complex document, but it is addressed to men and lays down a series of laws that they have to obey. It is they who are seen as the rulers of society. Yet Jewish culture was also more egalitarian to women than the Greek culture which increasingly dominated because of the Roman occupation. In the Greek culture Platonic dualisms were influential: men versus women, civilisation versus nature, reason and logic versus emotion, good versus evil, light versus darkness. In this line up men were associated with civilisation, reason, good and light; women with nature, emotion, evil and darkness. This meant that women were by nature irrational and untrustworthy, incapable of looking after themselves. It is a notion that is by no means dead.

Judaism had a counterbalance to seeing women as inferior because some of its sources emphasised complementarity: the Genesis creation story of woman being made from the man's rib can be seen as patriarchal, but it can also be seen as making the two complementary: men will never be complete without women and vice versa. Arguably as Christianity developed it had to convince the Roman world of its respectability and lack of threat and in the course of this the complementary nature of many Jewish sources lost ground against the platonic influence of Roman culture. It certainly seems to be the case that women played a much more prominent part in the very early church than later.[1]

We have seen above how Jesus engaged with, was challenged by, and learnt from the Canaanite woman. That was an example of Jesus responding outside the norms of the male-dominated society in which he lived.

A second example is in John's gospel, chapter 4 when he

1. Rodeheaver, op cit.

meets a woman from Samaria at a well. Like the Canaanite woman story, it is another example of diversity because Jesus being a Jew should not have been speaking to the woman on two counts: she was a Samaritan and Jews did not speak to Samaritans because they were enemies. Secondly, men did not speak to strange women or vice versa.

All the stories in John's gospel have many layers and one of the purposes of this story is to focus on Jesus as the new Covenant or agreement between God and humans. Part of the conflict between Jews and Samaritans was over the Temple being based in Jerusalem. This was important to Jews and rejected by the Samaritans. But Jesus at the end of the story is pointing to himself as the new Temple, the new mediator between God and humans.

Yet it is also important that John uses the figure of the woman as the means by which this message is communicated.

A third example is Mary of Magdala. She is often presented as a prostitute, although not in the scriptures. The mistake is made partly because people think she is the unnamed woman in Luke (7:36 ff) who brought perfume to Jesus and wet his feet with her tears, even though there is nothing in the text to suggest this. (This reading was used for her memorial in the pre-Vatican II missal.) A second reason for the false association is the 17th century painting by Giovanni Gioseffo dal Sole in which she is depicted gazing at the cross seemingly mindful of her sins. Because she is bare breasted and because of the patriarchal mindset dominant at the time the assumption was made that her sins must be sexual and so she must be a prostitute.

In fact the gospels tell us that Jesus cast out seven devils from her (Mark 16:9). This simply means that he healed her from some physical or psychological illness. We are not told the nature of the illness. She was one of the group of women that went around Galilee with Jesus. She was present at the Cross. She went to the tomb on the first Easter morning. And all four gospels list her as a witness to the resurrection. In both Matthew and John we are told that she met the risen Christ before any of the male apostles.

It is to St John in particular that we owe this picture of Magdalene. In one of the most beautiful passages in the New Testament (John 20:11-18) we are told that Mary went out to the tomb 'while it was still dark' on that first morning. When she arrived the heavy stone in front of the tomb had been rolled away. Two angels dressed in white were sitting inside. The body of Jesus is not there. They ask her why she is crying and she tells them that it is because they have taken away her lord and she does not know where they have put him.

She then turns around and sees the gardener standing there. He asks her why she is crying and 'Who is it that you are looking for?' This time instead of answering his question directly Mary says: 'If you took him away, sir, tell me where you have put him, and I will go and get him'.

Jesus then says one word to her – only one. That word transformed her life. Nothing was ever the same again for her. That word also changed my life, and yours, because of what Mary did after she heard the one word.

The word was a simple one: her name, Mary. Nothing else. Simply her name.

She knew him then, because her name was spoken to her by someone she knew and loved. John puts it simply: 'She turned towards him and said in Hebrew "Rabbuni", which means "Teacher".' She threw her arms around him.

Jesus tells her not to hold on to him 'because I have not yet gone back up to the Father' (John 20:17). For years this puzzled me. What else did he expect her to do? She loved him deeply. She had followed him in all his journeys in Palestine. She had been there in the good times and the bad. She had gone up with him to Jerusalem, knowing as well as anyone the dangers faced by a prophet in Jerusalem. She had almost certainly been there at the last supper and in the garden, although we are not told this. She would have seen the mockery of the trial, the baying for blood by the crowd, the way of the cross, and the brutality of the crucifixion. She would have heard his screams on the cross (men scream when they are in agony), and she would have seen the final collapse of the body in death.

Now, seeing him standing before her, apparently alive, she throws her arms around him and he tells her not to cling to him. What did he expect her to do? Indeed, as someone who loved her, what did he want to do himself?

Sandra Schneiders explains it in terms of the two times that

'turning' is used in the passage.[1] The first is when, after addressing the angels, she notices the gardener standing behind her and
turns around towards him. The literal translation is that 'she
turned toward the things that lie behind'. For Schnieders this
means that by focusing on the dead body of Jesus she is concent-
rating on what has past: the earthly life of Jesus which came to
an end on the cross. When Jesus calls her by her name he is calling one of his own – a reference to the Good Shepherd who
knows his sheep. He is calling her to turn away from the past
and towards the future.

Jesus resists her embrace because Mary in her mind is embracing the Jesus whom she knew in Palestine. It is the same
person before her, but now there is a difference: he is the Risen
Christ. Mary is looking to the past. Jesus is looking to the ever-
present future. She has to let go of the past, of the person she has
known in the past, to discover the same person as the person of
the future.

That letting-go, which he asks of her, means giving up not
just what she knew of the past, what she treasured so much and
longed for, but also letting go of the impossible joy which had
seized her when she realised he was alive. Unless he ascends to
the Father he cannot be with her as the Risen Christ, united with
the Father. Only when this happens can the Father send the
Spirit who is the Spirit of the love that the Father has for the Son
and the Son for the Father, to be with not only her, but all other
people in the world.

Yet more is asked of Mary: not only must she do all this letting-go. She also has to announce to the whole world that he is
risen. This is her privilege: she is the first to hear this news and
to bring it to others. John is the clearest of all the gospel writers
on the mission she receives. Mary thus fulfils the criteria for
being an apostle in the New Testament: she accompanied Jesus
in his earthly life, she saw the risen Lord, and she was commissioned to preach the gospel.[2]

So Mary of Magdala, one of the women who loved Jesus, and
was loved by him in turn, is the first to experience him as risen

---

1. Sandra M. Schneiders, *Written That You May Believe: Encountering
Jesus in the Fourth Gospel*, New York, Crossroad, 2003, 211 ff.
2. Schneiders, p. 237, Note 16.

and is commissioned by him to bring this news to the rest of the world. In presenting her in this way John, arguably, places her on at least an equal footing with Mary the mother of Jesus.

It is interesting to note that in the church's liturgical calendar there are at least 13 feasts for Mary the mother of God, celebrating this and other aspects of her life. There are none for Mary of Magdala. Instead she gets one memorial. That seems strange, but perhaps it reflects deeper currents which have been in the church, not since the beginning, but since early in its history. I suspect that we have made our God into a male God when in fact God is both male and female. Genesis tells us that God made humans in God's own image: 'male and female he made them' (Gen: 1:27). We have focused on the maleness in God. Have we also looked around for a place for the feminine in God and cast this on Mary the mother of God, forgetting that the definition of Mary as mother of Christ was a statement about Christ's full, unified humanity?

The gospels were written between 70 and approximately 90 AD, that is about 40-60 years after the death of Jesus. The prominence given to Mary Magdalene by all four writers, using different sources, suggests that she played a major role in the early church. This is particularly true in the case of St John. His gospel is highly theological: all the characters in it play a symbolic role, whatever about their actual historical role. John shows Jesus appearing first to Magdalene, itself significant. But she is then commissioned, given a task: she is to go to the other disciples and tell them the good news that Jesus is risen. The reason John wrote his gospel was that people would believe in the risen Christ. Mary is the first to hear this news, accept it, to be commissioned to proclaim it, and to actually proclaim it. She is therefore the first and only woman apostle. John Paul II, following Bernard of Clairvaux, called her the 'apostle of the apostles'.

In Jesus' life, then, in the fundamental moments of the revelation of his being alive after death, and in the life of the early church, it is clear that women played a leadership role. Jesus' message undermined all discrimination because it was about respect for all. So did his actions.

Superiority

We have mentioned that respect is a constant theme in every-thing that Jesus did and said, although, as we also saw he had to learn it partly through his encounter with the Canaanite woman. Another element of that respect is his fundamental op-position to any perceived superiority of one group over another.

Again and again, as we have seen, he chides the scribes and Pharisees for trying to show themselves as superior, letting peo-ple know that they were fasting, standing at street corners to pray, going to the front of the Temple to pray, taking the first places at weddings and having people call them 'Rabbi'. Jesus tells his followers that they must be different: 'You must not allow yourselves to be called Rabbi, since you have only one Master, and you are all brothers' (and sisters) (Mt 23:8). There is a basic equality in the Christian community. Titles, hierarchies, symbols of superiority, all these are radically challenged by this equality.

Deference

For the same reason there can be no deference in Christ's com-munity. People have different roles, but they are equal as per-sons. As we shall see, Paul, after his conversion and his commis-sioning by Christ as an apostle, does not consult with the leaders of the church in Jerusalem but straight away begins preaching the gospel. Later he does meet them, in order to explain what he is doing and also to consult with them about the difficult issue of Jewish-Gentile relationships within the church. In doing so he is recognising that they have a certain primacy. He persuades them to accept his view on the issue of diversity, and when Peter falls back from this position Paul has no hesitation in challeng-ing him. Respecting a role has nothing to do with personal def-erence.

Transparency

Children are transparent. When I was a child if I was being questioned about doing something wrong – and that seemed to happen a lot – I always did my best to put up a robust defence. But they always used an unfair weapon against me when they accused me of lying: they made me put out my tongue. And if there was a black mark on it, then they knew I was lying. There was always a black mark on my tongue! Mind you, I never saw it, and the few times I checked in the mirror it seemed to be gone. But they said it was there, every time.

We tend to lose black marks on our tongues as we get older. We learn to hide things. That is not a bad thing: it is appropriate to reveal things about ourselves to others only in accordance with the relationship we have with them. So when people ask how we are today we tend to answer 'Fine', unless they are close to us in which case the answer may be very different. Even if it is not, those close to us will probably know how we really are.

Jesus put little children before his disciples as examples of what he wanted them to be. This did not mean that he wanted them to revert to being infants. It had to do, probably, with transparency. It is closely related to honesty. It is the opposite of élite insiders in a group saying 'Tell them nothing' when referring to others in the group. It is about not doing one thing while pretending to do another.

The word 'hypocrisy' often comes up about the church because it turns out that priests and bishops do not always practise what they preach. This is not quite what transparency is about. No minister of the gospel practices all that she or he preaches, because no person is without sin. If we followed the logic of some who talk about hypocrisy we should only preach what we ourselves practise well. That might mean having to leave out a lot of the gospel and we are called to preach the full gospel. The issue raised by transparency is self-righteousness: if we preach the gospel without admitting our own sinfulness we are not transparent. We are not admitting the truth about ourselves. We are also putting ourselves above others. That is both wrong and foolish.

Accountability
Time after time Jesus reminded people that 'the hour is coming'. He told them to be prepared. There was an urgency in his message. If the householder had known at what hour the thief was coming he would have been prepared (Luke 12:39). The five wise virgins were prepared when they came to the house to wait for the bridegroom: they brought oil for their lamps. The five

foolish ones did not (Mt 25:1-13). The father asked two sons to go and work in the field. One said he would go and did not. The other said No, but went. The one who went, despite saying No, was the one who did the will of the Father (Mt: 21:28-32). At the last judgment scene the sheep are told that they did the will of the Father because they fed the hungry, they gave water to the thirsty, they welcomed the stranger, they clothed the naked, they visited those who were sick or in prison. Because of this they enter into their eternal reward. The goats who did not do these things are sent away to eternal punishment.

People need to be prepared because they will have to give an account of themselves.

Powerlessness
The greatest picture that Christians have of God is that presented by Christ in the New Testament: 'Whoever sees me, sees the Father' (Jn: 14:9) Jesus says to Phillip. People often think of God as all-powerful and indeed that is true. But it is also true, if we are to believe the New Testament, that God is powerless.

Jesus came that all might have life and have it to the full. He wanted an end to illness, oppression, marginalisation and violence. He wanted people to use their talents. He wanted us to realise our capacity to overcome our fears, to care for one another, in short, to love each other.

In the temptations he was offered the use of power to achieve his ends: 'Turn this stone into bread' (Lk 4: 3). He wanted people to have enough to eat. Being one with God he had the capacity to turn all stones into food. The story is an image of the fullness of life that he wanted people to have. It is told in three of the gospels. The gospel writers would have avoided it had they been able to do so: the best way to present a biography of a hero that one is trying to build up is not to show him being tempted. But clearly this was something that happened throughout Jesus' life. We see echoes of the same temptation when he tells the disciples that he is going to suffer and be crucified when he goes to Jerusalem. Peter loyally springs to his defence. For his troubles Jesus snaps at him: 'Get behind me, Satan' (Mt 16:23). It is an extraordinary response unless we see it as that of a person deeply troubled, trying to find his way forward, seeing the path of the cross ahead of him and trying to find another. In that context he snaps at his friend – because friends are people to whom we can safely express our fears and anger. This is not a picture of an all-powerful God.

When we move forward to the Agony in the Garden we see a man on his knees collapsing and shaking, sweating blood in his dread.

On the cross the bystanders jeered him: 'He cured others. Let him now save himself.'

There was no rescue from the cross. There was no magic from heaven. The stones were not turned into bread. People were not forced to follow Jesus: he left it to our choice. He desperately wants us to make the right choice. He knows the wrong choice will harm us. But he will not impose his will on us. God, in Christ, has handed over God's power to us. We can live as Christ wants us to, or we can choose the opposite. It turns out that the all-powerful God has given up God's power.

In the readings for the feast of Christ the King for year C, the first reading is from 2 Samuel and shows the appointment of David as the King of the Jewish tribes. This gave him power, authority, status and money. The second reading, from Colossians 1, tells us of the power of Christ: 'For in him were created all things in heaven and earth.' He is 'the first in every way'. But the gospel of that day shows us the reality of God's power in Christ: a broken piece of flesh hanging on the cross as a criminal. That is a picture of powerlessness. Yet it is also a picture of the greatest power the world has ever seen. It is the power of God's love which will ultimately overcome evil in us, not by force, but by invitation.

We are called as a people

All these qualities championed by Jesus are related. Because people are to be respected there is a fundamental equality between them. That means there can be no superiority or deference. There needs to be a fundamental honesty which challenges deviousness or inappropriate secrecy. There is a need for respect for diversity because people differ in their personalities, culture, religion and talents. Men and women are fundamentally equal, so gender and all other forms of discrimination are wrong.

These challenges by Our Lord are not only to us as individuals, but also to us as a people. We saw in the Old Testament how important it was that God dealt with the Jews both as individuals and as the Chosen People. Christians, the younger brothers and sisters of the Jews, also face that challenge.

In the Old Testament the patriarchs and prophets were often the mediators between God and the people. This is not an absolute pattern. We saw that Moses went out to the Tent of Meeting to speak with Yahweh as a man talks to his friend. But we are also told that all the people, when they wanted to consult with Yahweh themselves, also went out to the tent. So there was a hierarchical structure, but it was not absolute.

In the New Testament there is an important change: Jesus tells people that he is the way, the truth and the life. When people see him, they see the Father. Jesus replaces all other mediators. But he also tells us to talk to his Father directly, as when he taught his disciples to pray: 'Our Father ...' People are therefore called to be intimate with the Father directly. (The word Jesus uses for his Father 'Abba', might more accurately be translated as 'Da' or 'Daddy' because this conveys more of the intimacy suggested by the word.) But we are also called to be intimate with Jesus himself: our personal relationship with him is at the centre of what it is to be a Christian. Indeed, without this nothing else in the faith makes much sense.

Yet the word 'Father' or 'Abba' is only one of the two first words in the Our Father. The other word is 'Our'. God is the Father/Mother of a people. It is as a people that we are called to address God. It is always tempting to forget this, to try to go to God alone, to focus on me and Jesus. But that is not Christianity. Christ calls us as a people as well as individuals.

Jesus seems to have given people different roles, although we need to be tentative in all our claims, since it is difficult to be definite about scriptural analysis. One group is the Twelve apostles. They are mentioned several times, and as we shall see the early church saw the need to choose a replacement for Judas. Yet their names vary in different lists in different gospels. Later Paul would claim to be an apostle. And John, in his gospel, portrays Mary Magdalene as the first of the apostles, as we have seen.

Secondly, we are told that 72 were sent out in pairs to proclaim Christ. We have no names for them. Thirdly, there is frequent mention of 'his disciples'. Each of these groups seems distinct from the wider group of 'the people' to whom he preached and whom he often healed. However, it would be wise to be cautious in drawing firm conclusions from these structures. It is not always clear which were set up by Christ and which were developed later by the early church.

Uncertainty

The social function of religion is to help people deal with the uncertainty caused by unanswerable questions. We all crave certainty. It gives us security. This is one reason why Jesus was so opposed to religion when it is based on external ritual in the absence of relationships.

Again and again he told people that the kingdom of heaven – the new community that God is bringing about – was like different things – a mustard seed which grows into a great tree, yeast that a woman puts into bread to make it rise – but he never told them exactly what it was. This is because this new community will be in the hands of God and God is a mystery. The call of Jesus is from certainty to uncertainty, from the known to the unknowable, from clarity to mystery.

Failure of Christ

In reality Jesus failed in his mission. Or so it seemed. In his own time many did not respect others. The authorities who were fundamentally challenged by the radical nature of his teaching responded with violence and killed him. Groups continued to try to dominate others.

Jesus wanted the qualities he preached to be practised above all by his church because the church is called to show the presence of God in the world. He would be deeply disappointed in this as well because the church will always be a sinful institution. The clerical child abuse is a deeply shameful example of this. But it is only one of many throughout the centuries.

Yet, despite the apparent failure of his mission and our own failure to follow the gospels, Christians celebrate the victory of Christ. That is what Christian hope is about.

Christian hope is not based on some naïve notion that human beings will finally start living as we are meant to. It is fundamentally realistic: Christ knows what we are like. Anyone with the slightest knowledge of the wars of the 20th century should have no illusions about our capacity for evil. Yet God, in Christ, continues to love us, to call us, and to hope that we will respond.

That in part is what the cross was about. Christ entered into his passion which at one level represented the complete failure of his mission: the people he loved, whom he had come to call into the fullness of Christ, responded by seeking to destroy him. That knowledge was part of the reason why we are given the picture of Christ being broken in the garden of Gethsemane. He broke down, wept and sweated blood. He begged his Father to rescue him. It is worth asking: what did he want the Father to rescue him from? Part of the answer is: from living human life to the full.

That phrase 'living life to the full' is often used in silly contexts, such as applying it to a heavy drinker who spends his time partying and drinking. He is not living life to the full because he is avoiding life by numbing his brain. This is not to suggest that celebration is not part of Christian living. Of course it is. But so are many other things, mostly focused on using our talents to love other people. In the case of Christ the temptation was to walk away, to avoid the reality, to give up preaching the message, to flee from Jerusalem, to live an 'ordinary' life, above all to run away from loving his Father and loving other people. The victory of Christ is that he did not run. Instead he chose, not only to live life to the full, but to show us how to do so ourselves. Our hope springs from the fact that not only has one like ourselves succeeded in doing this, but that he calls us, no matter how often we fail, to do the same ourselves. Our hope is also that, massive though the pain and suffering caused by our sins is, the love of God in Christ is more powerful still.

`If God is for us, who can be against us? Since he did not spare his own Son, but gave him up for the sake of all of us, then can we not expect that with him he will freely give us all his gifts?' (Roms 8:31-32).

Conclusion

If faith was about certainty there would be no need for it. If we could take the 'if' out of statements about God then life would be easier. Or so it seems. In reality if we could do that God would no longer be a mystery. Rather God would be one more element of life that we could seek to dominate. But precisely because God is a mystery whom we can never understand, that 'if' about God's existence and who God is remains in place.

Faith is always a struggle. There are days and moments when God seems present, many when this is not the case. We can and should search within ourselves, our relationships and our wider lives for glimpses of this fleeting presence. But Christianity is about more than our personal experience, although if we are to relate to it we can only do so by finding some connection with our own experience. Part of what lies beyond ourselves is the scriptures, that peculiar, contradictory, mysterious, but also deeply attractive series of books and letters that emerged over the course of nearly 3000 years. In this section I have touched on some passages that mean a lot to me. That meaning grew slowly. For many years much of the scriptures was closed to me. I found it boring, contradictory, irrelevant to my life. That is still the case with many parts of it. The meaning that I found in some of it came through retreats, theology, and eventually seeing some connections between these passages and the lives of myself and others.

The picture of Moses – in parts – and of Christ that emerges from the scriptures is deeply attractive to me. With Moses it is a picture of someone who grew in his relationship with God until eventually he could sit and share with him as a man does with his friend. With Christ it is a picture of a passionate lover, who precisely because he was a lover was outraged by injustice, and yet was also filled with a never-ending compassion. That compassion did not blind him to our injustices. Instead it led him to confront us, take on himself the fury of our hatred, and invite us into a new relationship with him and with others. It was a compassion that led him through the cross to the hope of the resurrection. Our hope as Christians is not one that denies human wrong or suffering, but one that faces evil and yet still believes that the love of God is even more powerful.

That picture of Christ for me fits in with those moments, however brief, of experiences of the presence of God.

It does not remove the doubts of faith. For me, as for many others, faith can be in part an experience of being pursued by God. The silence becomes too frustrating, the demands of living life to the full become too great – or so we think – and we turn to lesser things to escape. We can be like Augustine, at least in part:

Late have I loved you, O Beauty ever ancient, ever new,
late have I loved you!
You were within me, but I was outside,
and it was there that I searched for you.
In my unloveliness I plunged into the lovely things which you created.
You were with me, but I was not with you.
Created things kept me from you;
yet if they had not been in you they would have not been at all.
You called, you shouted, and you broke through my deafness.
You flashed, you shone, and you dispelled my blindness.
You breathed your fragrance on me;
I drew in breath and now I pant for you.
I have tasted you, now I hunger and thirst for more.
You touched me, and I burned for your peace.[1]

We search for beauty, truth, love, but so often in the wrong places or way.

Of course it is possible that all this is a silly dream, based on what we hope for. We may be like the child forever seeking to flee the parent, but running back for security. Certainly we never lose our neurotic tendencies. But psychology, useful as it is, has its limits. It is something like looking at the map of a country, which is useful, but different from loving a woman or a man within the country.

The following themes have emerged in this chapter:

- Friendship with God
- Compassion
- Justice
- God's forgiveness

---

1. *Confessions*, Book 10, Chapter 27.

- Diversity
- Respect
- Male domination
- Superiority
- Deference
- Transparency
- Accountability
- Power and powerlessness

These issues matter if we are to relate to God. Not surprisingly, they are also important if we are to be fully human. The call to us, however, goes beyond dealing within ourselves as individuals: we are also called to respond to them with others, many of whom differ from ourselves, within the church.

That is something I often want to avoid: it is too difficult. I want those who differ from me to go away. I want the church to be the way I want it. I do not want the church to be sinful. And the church stubbornly resists my desires. So, the struggle to believe in God, the struggle to experience God in our lives, the search for a God in the scriptures – a search that can often be confusing – needs another dimension: the search for God in the church.

That makes things even more difficult and confusing. But against our temptations to resist it, to run away from it lies the call of Christ. And, so far, that call has persisted with me, even though it has often been a close call.

In Section One we saw how parts of the church responded to the abuse crisis with values directly opposed to those of the Old and the New Testament. And so, I come to the second test which I need to answer if I am to remain in the Catholic church: given the values of the Old and New Testament how do I respond to church structures as they are revealed by the abuse crisis? Do they reflect the actual values of Christ in the New Testament? Or are they opposed to these values? But before discussing these I need to pause and ask a prior question: what is the church?

What is the Church – Ideal and Reality?

CHAPTER FIVE

What is the church?

Traditionally, the four marks of the true church were that it was one, holy, catholic and apostolic. Each of these is important, as we shall see, but it is perhaps more important to start by asking what is the purpose of the church. There are several aspects to the answer.

Varieties of church

The church means different things to different people. Most media attention concentrates on popes, bishops, priests and abuse. Older Catholics often focus on going to Sunday or daily Mass – although most are also furious at some church leaders for their response to abuse. Parish clergy may be caught up in visiting the sick, administering the sacraments, repairing buildings and wondering what to do about the schools they manage, and trying to keep their morale up as many others see them also as abusers. Church can mean frequent devotional confession. Or it can mean someone coming into a church building after years searching for meaning elsewhere and finding new depths. Church can be a small group of religious coming together for prayer, worship, fun, a meal and support. Or it can be a term of identity: 'We're Catholics' (which may mean we are not like 'those Protestants or Jews '). Or it may be seen as a large, seemingly united organisation dedicated to the overthrow of Protestantism (the view of some Northern Ireland Protestants). Or it can be an empty, cold building that offers nothing.

Being a 'good Catholic' for many means 'I should go back to Sunday Mass and start saying the Rosary again, as my parents did.'

For others it means trying somewhat desperately to remain part of an institution where one's faith has been nourished but where almost every aspect of the institution, from the exclusion of women, to the monarchical papacy, to a poor parish experience which grates like sandpaper on an open wound. For others, the parish can be a lively, energetic community where their faith is nourished.

WHAT IS THE PURPOSE OF THE CHURCH?

*The church is a coming together of followers of Christ to share good
news and to connect with each other.*

The church did not start as an abstract idea. It started as an experience of Christ shared by a group of people. That experience
turned their lives upside down.

Near the beginning of his gospel John tells the story of John
the Baptist pointing Jesus out to two of his disciples and telling
them: 'Look, there is the lamb of God' (Jn 1: 36). The two disciples follow him. Jesus turns around and asks them: 'What do
you want?' It is one of the deepest questions that we can be
asked. John's two disciples are obviously thrown by the question and respond with their own: 'Where do you live?' Jesus invites them to come and see. We are told they spent the rest of the
day with him and from that day forth their lives were changed.
Nothing was ever the same again. As Andrew, one of them, told
his brother Simon: 'We have found the Messiah'. This was an experience that they could not keep to themselves.

They came together because it is natural for people who have
had an ecstatic experience to seek out others who have gone
through something similar.

In some intuitive way the early Christians experienced themselves as a group, as belonging together. They had had this relationship with Jesus before his death. They felt drawn to him and
to follow him. Now, after his death, they had an encounter with
him which they described as his 'Resurrection', in which they
experienced him as living, still the same person, but in a different way. On its own this experience did not transform them.

We are told in the gospels that after the death of Jesus some
of his followers fled to the country. Two of them met a stranger
on the road who asked them why they were so upset. They were
amazed at the question, since the whole country was talking
about Jesus, about the great prophet he had been, how he had
been handed over by the Jewish leaders to the Roman authorities to be crucified, and how they themselves had hoped 'that he
was the one who was going to redeem Israel' (Lk 24:21). Clearly
they had since lost all that hope. They even told the stranger
about some of the women in their group who claimed to have

had a vision of angels who told them that he was alive.

In the story the stranger acts as if he is going to continue on his journey when they get to Emmaus, but they persuade him to stay with them. While he was with them he took the bread, broke it, said the blessing and gave it to them. At that moment they recognised him as Jesus. Immediately, we are told, they got up and rushed back to Jerusalem. Why? To tell the others in their group the incredible news that they had experienced Jesus as living. It was news that they had to share with others. The news, literally, burst out of them. In the first instance that meant sharing it with people within their own group.

The church is a means of sharing good news with other people
The good news on its own did not transform the early Jewish followers of Christ. The disciples remained locked in the upper room in Jerusalem because they were afraid for their lives, understandably so in view of what had happened to Jesus. It was not until the descent of the Holy Spirit at Pentecost that they were transformed. Then they burst out of the room and started shouting about their experiences all over the city.

What was this experience that changed them so deeply? What was it that changed so many sceptics (Peter, the women, the disciples on the road to Emmaus, Thomas, Paul) into fervent believers, even though some, like Paul, were clearly deeply committed to their already existing Jewish faith? What was it that transformed them from terrified wimps, running away from Jerusalem, or locked into that upper room, into crazy, seemingly drunk preachers – as some thought who heard them? Peter responded that they could not be drunk because it was only 9.00 in the morning (Acts 2:15) a comment that made Raymond Brown, the late Catholic biblical scholar, facetiously remark that Peter did not know much about drinking. What is the experience that even today convinces so many people, from such different backgrounds and personalities, that nothing is more important in the world than following Christ? What is it about that experience that calls people into communities, however inadequate and sinful these are?

It burst out of them on that first day of Pentecost, but it continued bursting out after that until it spread in one form or another to most parts of the planet. Over time the process of telling the good news would be refined. People would learn that culture was important. (Actually this lesson was already present in that first Pentecost scene, because each one present heard the message in his or her own language.) As part of this they would learn to distinguish between essential and non-essential parts of the message and about their own biases. They would begin to understand the importance of dialogue and that the preacher is likely to learn as much about Christ from the listener as vice versa. All this learning would take time, much struggle and conflict.

In the church, teaching about God can be formulated

As Jews – and almost all the first Christians were Jewish – the early church wanted to worship God in a new way: through Jesus Christ. That was a great and difficult change for them because it challenged – or seemed to challenge – two central beliefs of Jews: one was that God is one. To say that Jesus is one with God suggests that there are two persons in God and that God is therefore not one. It took several hundred years for the community to work out a statement of belief that there are three persons in God, Father, Son and Holy Spirit, and that God is nonetheless one.

The second Jewish belief challenged by worshipping God through Jesus was that God is utterly transcendent: how can this be so if Jesus, a human like us, is one with God? Again the community slowly worked out the statement that Jesus is both fully human and fully divine at the same time.

These belief statements took a long time to formulate. The words of the formula only emerged because people kept meeting, praying, thinking and talking about their experience over several hundred years. It was not only good motives and experiences that led to the wording people used at the Council of Nicaea in 325. The Emperor, a non-believer, locked them into a room and kept them there until they came up with an agreed answer. He was not particularly concerned what the answer was. He simply wanted to stop divisions within the Empire that impacted on his interests.

The church is a place in which people come together to worship
The early disciples came together because they wanted not only to pray but also to pray together. St Cyprian says:

> Above all, the Teacher of peace and Master of unity did not want prayer to be made singly and privately, so that whoever prayed would pray for himself alone. We do not say 'My Father, who art in heaven' or 'Give me this day my daily bread'; nor does each one ask that only his own debt should be forgiven him; nor does he request for himself alone that he may not be led into temptation but delivered from evil. Our prayer is public and common, and when we pray, we pray not for one person but for the whole people, since we, the whole people, are one.[1]

Another reason was because the Eucharist seems to have been at the centre of the early meetings of the church. Paul (1 Cor 11:23-26) tells us he had been told that the Lord at the Last Supper took bread, said the blessing, gave it to them and said: 'Do this in memory of me'; and did the same with the cup. From the very early days the church seems to have done the same. But they did so as a group.

In time of course the church would have horrendous conflicts over the meaning of the Eucharist. It was one of many reasons that led to the splits in Christendom which we call the Reformation. Two bad results of these splits were that Protestants tended to focus on the scriptures and Catholics on the Eucharist and each neglected the other. Fortunately these tendencies are fading, however slowly, as theologians in different churches work together to learn from each other. Yet, while Eucharistic sharing with Protestants is allowed within the Roman Catholic church on occasion, it is far too infrequent, given the unity that already exists.

For many Catholics the Eucharist is at the centre of their belief. The following is one person's testimony:

> The Eucharist has always been central to my Christian faith. From about the age of three, I remember my mother bringing me and my brother to daily Mass which was very important to her. I remember we sat at the front near the altar and she would tell us that God loved us very much, that he was

---

1. St. Cyprian, Treatise Four, *The Lord's Prayer*, Ch 8.

always looking after us even though we couldn't see him, and that he was present on the altar at Mass. She said he was always present in the tabernacle and that the red light was a sign to tell us he was always there.

As a child I listened intensely to her story and when the priest at Mass opened the tabernacle, everything was so dazzling white inside that I knew somebody very special and good was there. Through that daily visit I came to know that he loved me even when I was bold. That sense of presence has remained ever since and has been the most important constant in my life.

That simple experience of a child grew as did my relationship with God until the real presence took hold inside me. I grew to love the Eucharist because it represented a way for me to celebrate this loving God that makes himself present or real in my life and those around me.

It was a very individualist approach to the Eucharist. It was about me deepening my relationship with God and feeling very gifted to be able to do this.

In my adult life the Eucharistic is much more about a communal relationship with God. It is an experience of coming together with people from various walks of life, young and old, sick and well, rich and poor, good and bad, to share with God who becomes present in our midst. For me as adult it is more an experience of being part of the Trinity – the love of the Father for the Son poured out on the community of believers through the Holy Spirit. In the Eucharist I feel a living part of the Trinity.

As a community we listen to the word of God, we open ourselves to the Holy Spirit, we share the meal in memory and in celebration. We pray for each other as a community and we leave with a spirit of solidarity to help those around us as best we can. It is a daily commitment to 'go forth in peace to love and serve the Lord'. I have a great sense that we are all part of the Body of Christ, that he loves each and everyone of us in a unique and special way and that we each have a special mission to live out.

My mission is to be a living witness to Christ in the world by the way I live my life and do my work – something that is never easy to do.

The church is meant to be a sign of the presence of God in the world
God is a mystery but we know some things about that mystery. For the Christian the best image or picture of God is Jesus. Jesus is the human face of God. If you want to know what God looks like look at Jesus. That picture shows us someone with compassion, humour, anger, depth, commitment, an openness to being challenged, a willingness to suffer and a great belief not only in humanity but in each individual. He was also someone who focused on outsiders – the tax collectors who oppressed the people terribly and colluded with the Roman occupiers, thereby polluting the holy places of the Jews, the prostitutes who in the view of that patriarchal society led men astray, the widow who put all the little cash she had into the Temple.

If the church was to show the presence of Jesus in the world today it would be a fun church with a lot of celebration – Jesus spent a lot of time eating and drinking with people. It would certainly not be a comfort zone for like minded people – Jesus was not great at social manners: he allowed a prostitute wipe his feet with her tears when he was having a meal at the house of Simon the Pharisee (Luke 7:36). It would be an angry church – the clearing of the Temple is but one example of the fury of Jesus when he saw people mistreated. It would be a church of hope – Jesus faced into the depths of human evil, was faithful to his Father, to us and to life, and came out the other end intact as a human being, alive and reunited with the Father.

The church is meant to be a service of compassion and respect for sinners
If the church was to follow the example of Our Lord it certainly would be a place of compassion and understanding for sinners – the gospels are full of stories of Jesus reaching out to people in trouble. And there were no limits to that reaching out. Today it would include both those who were abused by clergy and those who abused. That can sometimes be hard news for those who have been wronged. Their understandable response is discussed in the story of the Prodigal Son.[1] The real point of the story is that there are no lengths to which God will not go to connect with people who want to separate themselves from God by doing wrong to others. It is highly significant that at the end

---

1. Brian Lennon SJ, *So You Can't Forgive? Moving Towards Freedom*, Dublin, Columba, 2009.

of the story the Father is positioned outside the feast, standing alongside the elder brother who would not go into the feast because he was so angry at the Father receiving his younger brother back into the family. The Father has indeed welcomed the younger brother back – he ran to meet him, threw his arms around him, covered him with kisses, and held a great feast in his honour. But now having made sure that the younger brother has been restored to the family he is worried about the elder brother, and so he will stay outside the house with the elder brother until he too comes to his senses and rejoins the family.

There are dangers with every text. One danger with this one is for the church to read it as if the church is the family of God, those who are separated from us are all sinners, and only when they return to the bosom of the church – as represented by us – will they be saved. But the story is not about people coming back to the church. It is about people coming back to Christ. Yes, the church is meant to represent the presence of Christ in the world. But many people cannot see this. This is not because they are stupid or sinful. It is at least partly because we in the church are often stupid or sinful. Further, the story of the Prodigal Son is not about the Father threatening his sons but about his respecting their freedom, going out to meet them, listening not to their words but to their actions, not imposing anything on them, but rejoicing in them as they are, and in the end being with them no matter what their situation was.

During the Troubles in Northern Ireland bishops and priests, including myself, together with many lay people, condemned violence by the IRA because it was wrong. We were right to do so. It was also important that we condemned loyalist and state violence when the latter was wrong. But our capacity to make an impact by such condemnations was limited by two factors. One was our relationship with those who were committing the violence: were we involved with their lives and their world? Did we care about what happened to them? Did they see us as 'on their side' in terms of their real interests of jobs, security, etc? Or did they see us as outsiders siding with the enemy? While it is important to recognise the bias among supporters of violence, our capacity to challenge effectively the terrible wrong of violence, from whatever quarter, greatly depended on our relationship with those carrying it out.

The church is meant to bring the justice of God to the world

Latin American liberation theology which emerged during the conflicts of the 1970s, along with other theologies, emphasised how much our reading of the scriptures depends on our context. For example, in the 1990s a group of Jesuits and colleagues met with local people in Ballyfermot, a marginalised area of Dublin, for a series of dialogue about the scriptures. One of the texts they looked at was the story of the ten talents (Mt: 25:14-30). In the parable one man is give ten talents, invests it and makes ten more. Similarly with the man who is given five talents. But the one who got only one talent went off and buried it. He says, 'I was afraid of you, because you are a hard man. You take out what you did not put in and reap what you did not sow' (Luke 19:21).

Most people respond to the parable by focusing on the guy with the ten talents and seeing it as an encouragement for all of us to use the gifts we have to make the world better for others. But when the group discussed the text one of the local women said that she identified with the man who buried the one talent, because if she had had the money she was afraid that she would have wasted it on useless things instead of spending it on things that really mattered.

There is a strand of Protestant theology, especially in the US, which focuses on riches being a reward from God for good living. This means that you get to be rich and righteous at the same time. It also means that if you are poor then clearly you are not right with God.

Jesus himself may not have been poor (there are disputes about this). His father was a carpenter which would have given him a role in society and some money. He was knowledgeable about the scriptures which meant that he may have been a rabbi or Pharisee, or if not that he managed to get education. He spent a lot of time hanging around with well-off people – most of the fellowship meals he took part in would have been hosted by them. Yet he saw his own calling in terms of liberating the oppressed: 'The Spirit of the Lord is upon me, because he appointed me to preach the gospel to the poor. He has sent me to proclaim release to the captives, and recovery of sight to the blind, to set free those who are downtrodden, to proclaim the favourable year of the Lord ... Today this scripture has been ful-filled in your hearing.' (Lk 4:18-21).

'Did not God choose the poor of this world to be rich in faith and heirs of the kingdom which he promised to those who love him?' (James 2:5).

He also clearly had an intense bond with people who were not well-off and he consistently challenged those who depended on wealth or saw themselves as better human beings because they were rich.

He told the parable of the man who put up more buildings on his farm in order to get richer, but died that night (Lk 12: 16-21). He said that the rich would find it harder to get into heaven than for a camel to get through the eye of a needle (Lk 18: 25). He often invited people to give everything they had to the poor and to follow him (Lk 18: 22). He saw the poor as blessed 'for theirs is the kingdom of heaven' (Mt 5: 3). He told the story of the rich man and Lazarus: Lazarus used to sit at the rich man's gate. Then both he and the rich man died. Lazarus went to heaven, the rich man to Hades. Yet the rich man had done nothing wrong: we are not told that he had caused Lazarus' poverty. For all we know from the story Lazarus was a wino. Yet the rich man ended up in Hades. Why? Because he did nothing. Because he did not see Lazarus as part of his community. Precisely be-cause of this he could have no part in the community of God. He told the parable of the Last Judgement in which people are again condemned to Hades: 'For I was hungry and you gave me noth-ing to eat, I was thirsty and you gave me nothing to drink, I was a stranger and you did not invite me in, I needed clothes and you did not clothe me, I was sick and in prison and you did not look after me' (Mt 25: 31-46).

Jesus was not making up a new doctrine in all this. One of the great themes of the Old Testament is the Covenant Community. The Chosen People are the Covenant Community. Their identity springs from God having chosen them as his own. Yet a condi-tion of their membership of the community is that they treat widows and orphans with respect:

If there is a poor man among you, one of your brothers, in any of the towns of the land which the Lord your God is giving you, you shall not harden your heart, nor close your hand to your poor brother; but you shall freely open your hand to him, and generously lend him sufficient for his need in whatever he lacks (Deut 15:7).

Now when you reap the harvest of your land, you shall not reap to the very corners of your field, neither shall you gather the gleanings of your harvest. Nor shall you glean your vineyard, nor shall you gather the fallen fruit of your vineyard; you shall leave them for the needy and for the stranger. I am the Lord your God (Lev 19:9 ff).

Is this not the fast which I choose, to loosen the bonds of wickedness, to undo the bands of the yoke, and to let the oppressed go free, and break every yoke? Is it not to divide your bread with the hungry, and bring the homeless poor into the house; when you see the naked, to cover him, and not to hide yourself from your own flesh?' (Is 58:6 ff).

The Old Testament was severe on those who abused the poor in the courts:

You hate the one who reproves in court
and despise him who tells the truth.
You trample on the poor
and force him to give you grain.
Therefore, though you have built stone mansions,
you will not live in them;
though you have planted lush vineyards,
you will not drink their wine.
For I know how many are your offences
and how great your sins.
You oppress the righteous and take bribes
and you deprive the poor of justice in the courts.
Therefore the prudent man keeps quiet in such times,
for the times are evil.
Seek good, not evil,
that you may live
(*Amos 5:10-14*).

The early church was committed to respect the marginalised. Luke puts the Magnificat in the mouth of Mary, the Mother of God. 'He has filled the hungry with good things but has sent the rich away empty' (Lk 1:53). In Acts we are told that all shared their wealth (2:45).

Traditionally the marks of the true church were that it was one, holy, catholic and apostolic. They are still important.

The church is meant to be One
In his account of the Last Supper St John puts a prayer for unity in the mouth of Jesus:

> I pray also for those who will believe in me through their message, that all of them may be one, Father, just as you are in me and I am in you. May they also be in us so that the world may believe that you have sent me (John 17:20-21).

Unity among his followers mattered to Our Lord. Yet churches remain divided. We go our separate ways on Sundays to worship despite the work done by theologians over 100 years to develop greater understanding of the issues that divided us. That work has borne fruit in the many agreed documents between churches. For decades leading theologians have asked if the divisions among us are so great that we are justified in remaining separate. We need strong and clear reasons to justify our remaining separate, given Our Lord's desire for unity.

Thankfully, interchurch relations in Northern Ireland in 2012 were incomparably better than 20 years previously. This reflects the reduction in tensions because of the peace process. But it also happened because so many clergy and lay people from different churches worked together during the Troubles to build understanding. In that joint work we came to understand each other personally much better and also got greater insights into the ecclesial and political worlds in which we lived. But as long as we worship separately on Sundays we have a long way to go.

It should also be recognised that one of the good things about the Roman Catholic church is its unity. Despite obvious differences, most Catholics are united about many issues, for example, the importance of the Eucharist (although the church's stated inability to ordain women is a block for many because of gender issues), the need for the church to be committed to justice, and the need to apply principles of justice within as well as outside the church.

The church is meant to be holy

Holiness means belonging to, being devoted to and empowered by God. That means living the sort of life that Our Lord led. Holiness, then, is not primarily to do with going to church, or even with prayer. Holiness, in the first place, means treating others with respect. That was at the centre of Christ's life. For him it also meant worshipping God. But worshipping God itself includes treating others with respect. The Old Testament constantly tells of Yahweh rejecting sacrifices because they are offered by people who act unjustly, as we have seen above. So justice is not an add-on to holiness. It is intrinsic to it.

Worship also involves turning to God directly, as God's people, giving God the reverence that is due to God.

Being holy is difficult for an individual, infinitely more so for an organisation. The church, because it is made up of human beings, will constantly fail in this task. But the call to seek holiness remains. That means prayer, worship, communal relationships and service of others similar to that of Our Lord's.

The church is meant to be catholic

'Catholic' means universal. The church is not meant to be a club of like-minded people. That is why I started this section by outlining some of the many different ways in which groups can be church.

I think this is one area in which the emphasis of my own church has been good. Catholics who go to Mass believe that they can do so in any part of the world, even if they do not understand the language. It is still the same Eucharist, the same remembrance of the once-for-all giving of Christ of himself with all the world to the Father.

Many Protestant churches have a different emphasis: they tend to focus on their local congregation. Some Presbyterians will worship only in the congregation of which they are a member. In doing so they have one advantage over Catholics: they can offer a more intimate experience of group support. But a disadvantage is the lack of universality that should be present in the church. Of course many Protestant churches emphasise this universality as well as Catholics.

Diversity is central to catholicity. Here all our churches fail. Church-goers tend to be middle-class. The Catholic church used to have better contacts with working-class groups but this has declined greatly.

'Catholic' also means being inclusive of young and old, rich and poor, conformer and non-conformer, able and disabled, people with differing sexual orientations, those with special needs and others, and different cultures. Being faithful to this is incredibly difficult because almost every church group is dominated by a small insider group who may well want to include others but either try to do so and fail or do not try at all.

Yet for the church to be the church it needs to be catholic or universal. One of the good things about the Roman Catholic church is that it is a worldwide organisation. In some ways this is an aspect of the church which has improved in recent decades because of globalisation.

The church is apostolic

The church is not a free flowing cell that emerged from nowhere. It is a group with a history and tradition. Catholics cannot suddenly decide that there are seven persons in the Blessed Trinity, because the faith that we have been handed on tells us there are three. Yes, we can and need to probe the meaning of faith statements. Yes, it is right that we should have many disagreements about, for example, what the word 'person' meant in the early ecumenical councils of the 4th and 5th centuries and what it means now. Yes, historical research will throw up many questions about, for example, the historical Jesus and the early Christian followers. But there is a basic content to the faith that cannot be changed.

As well as deciding on the original and current meaning of doctrinal formulas a second problem is deciding what doctrines need to be included in the basic content of the faith. How does the community decide this? In a slow development over several centuries some teachings about God and Christ were accepted and some rejected. That raises a fundamental question for the church: what is legitimate authority? And it is to that issue that we now turn.

CHAPTER SIX

Authority in the church

THE SCRIPTURES

Introduction

Why address the issue? After the Murphy and Ryan Reports on abuse pressure on the institutional church to reform became enormous. Five bishops in Ireland had resigned or offered to do so by the end of 2010; two of these resignations were rejected by the Vatican. Every session of the Bishops' Conference devoted considerable time to the issue. Groups of people who had been abused were deeply critical of the hierarchy and the Vatican. Many dioceses and religious congregations had paid large sums of money to abused people, and faced further claims. Legal efforts to sue the Vatican were being made.

Along with this there were continued calls for inclusion of lay people, especially women, in decision-making structures in the church.

There were other criticisms. Many found the church authoritarian: by this they meant that they did not find its authority credible for some or all the following reasons: the lack of democracy in appointments, the hidden processes, the reliance on authority rather than reason in making judgments on issues such as birth control or women's ordination, the insistence on celibacy for some clergy, while others, such as Anglican clergy or those of Eastern Rite churches in union with Rome are free to marry, or the clericalism of the church.

The charge is also made that the church's practice of Human Rights is far inferior to that of many secular structures, despite the richness of Catholic social teaching. This charge needs to be taken seriously by a community committed to following Christ.

However, many others find the church attractive for some of the same reasons that others object to it. They believe, for example, in the way papal authority is currently exercised. They accept the teaching on birth control precisely because it is taught by the magisterium. They agree with the ban on the ordination of women because they see it as part of the tradition, etc.

This highlights the divisions that exist within the church. But the side that is broadly happy with current church structures dominates these arguments. The other is marginalised.

Some argue that looking for changes in the institutional church is a lost cause, because the institution is not democratic. This is an unexamined mantra. Yes, the current structure of the church is not democratic. That does not mean it has to be this way in the future. It is certainly not the way it has always been in the past, as we shall see. The church is constantly changing, whether we like it or not. In 2010 it was immensely different from 40 years previously. It will be different again in 2050.

Many who disagree with the structures and with aspects of the institution of the church survive by ignoring the institution. But this means that they make no contribution to the changes which are going to happen.

Disagreement about the structures of the church saps the energy of the community. Either people struggle about it which itself takes energy, or they ignore the issue which makes change unlikely. Either way, the energy and life of the community is dissipated.

Some critics argue that the current structure of the church is bound to fail. Their opponents disagree because they see the structure directly linked to the promise Christ made to St Peter that he would be with the church until the end of time. Arguably they have a more prosaic argument to support them: in an age of increasing uncertainty many long for clarity and certainty: authoritarian structures are more likely to give this security. So the current structure may attract more than it repels in the future.

Whatever our view of these issues, the divisions themselves dramatically reduce the effectiveness of the church as a sign of the presence of God in the world and dissipate the energy of the community away from the building up of God's community. Disputes over authority are central to this division.

In this section I will look at the powers of the papacy, bishops and lay people within the church and show some of the significant changes that have taken place in history. I will summarise current Catholic teaching on authority in the church and ask what are the consequences of this for good governance within the church. I will then ask how we can move forward given the significant divisions which exist in the church.

The powers of popes, bishops and laity

The emergence of Rome as the diocese with primacy happened gradually. Here I will refer only to some of the main changes.

The organisation of the church, the location of its governance, and the balance between centralised and local power changed many times over the centuries.

In Acts, Chapter 1, we are given an early account of how the church organised itself. The issue was the appointment of an apostle to replace Judas who had betrayed Our Lord. The initiative was taken by Peter who addressed the whole community of about one hundred and twenty people. After he had outlined the need for a replacement the whole community nominated two candidates, Barnabus Justus and Matthias. Having prayed they then drew lots and Matthias was appointed.

A second incident was a dispute between the Hellenists – the Greek speakers – who complained that the Jewish members of the community were taking more than their fair share of the food given to the community as a whole. In response to this we are told that the Twelve, not Peter, called a full meeting of the community and told them that it was not appropriate that the Twelve should be hampered in their duty to preach the gospel by dealing with issues like this. So they told the community that they themselves must pick seven men of good reputation to whom the Twelve could hand over issues like this. The whole community approved of this and then elected the seven men who were later known as deacons.

A third aspect of the early church is shown in the life of Paul. He tells us (Gals 1:11-24) that when he was converted he did not go to Jerusalem to see any of the leaders there, but instead went to Arabia and Damascus and immediately began to preach the gospel and found local churches. He did this because he got his commission to preach as an apostle, not from any other human being, but directly from God.

Three years later he did go to Jerusalem and stayed with Peter for fifteen days. He also saw James, the brother of the Lord, who was the leader of the Jerusalem community, but no one else. The other Christians therefore had never met him, but many had heard of his conversion and preaching.

Fourteen years later Paul again went to Jerusalem. This was a more formal meeting, now known as the Council of Jerusalem, and had to do with the dispute over treatment of Gentile members of the church. He brought Barnabas and Titus with him. They met the Jerusalem leaders in a private meeting – which presumably means that the whole church was not involved at this stage in their deliberations.

This shows Paul acting with a good deal of independence from the church in Jerusalem. But it also shows him recognising the need for unity.

A fourth aspect of the early church emerges in that same meeting between Paul and the wider community in Jerusalem. The conflict over demands to be made of Gentile converts shows how the early community responded to diversity.

The issue was a major one: what obligations should be imposed on gentiles who converted. It seems as if all the first Christians were Jews, like Jesus himself. For them the law had been given to them by Yahweh. It was the law that made them into a people. Keeping the law was their part of the Covenant or agreement with Yahweh.

The law also played an important cultural role in the context of a divided community occupied by the Romans. Groups responded in different ways to this occupation: the Pharisees opposed the Romans and focused on the law. As they saw it, this would keep the people united. The Scribes collaborated more with the Roman authorities: they took the view that they could not remove the Romans so they had to work with them. There was tension between the two groups in part because of their different response to occupation. Others, like Matthew, became tax collectors. These collected taxes on behalf of the Romans, paid the Romans what they had to, and kept the rest. In a context of great poverty they were hated because they took money from the people, they collaborated with the oppressors, and they colluded in polluting the holy places. The Zealots chose violence: Simon, one of the Apostles, may or may not have been one of their number.

In this context many of the religious leaders cared deeply about the law. Many, therefore, would have been shocked when Paul proposed that Gentiles should not be required to follow the

Jewish law about circumcision and dietary customs. It is difficult for us to imagine just how challenging this must have been to pious Jews. It might be equivalent to asking a committed Catholic today to accept that really we made a mistake about the Eucharist and so in future we should abolish the Mass.

In the end the church held a Council at Jerusalem. At this, as we have seen, Paul prevailed. But it is worth noting that it was James, the brother of the Lord and the leader of the community in Jerusalem, and not Peter, who gave the final ruling. So, although Peter was seen as leader of the apostles he did not rule in all situations. James led the church in Jerusalem, but Peter's role was very prominent: he is given a special leadership position by Christ (for example in Mt 16:16-19), and his position is also recognised by Paul. He also seems to have played an important role as a source for Mark's gospel.

What themes emerge from this brief summary of how the early church governed itself?

1. Communal involvement: While the leaders played key roles – Peter seems to have decided both that they needed a replacement for Judas and the criteria which should govern the selection, the Twelve decided that they should not be involved in sorting out rows over food distribution – the community as a whole played a role in many of the events: it was they who elected the candidates to replace Judas and they also selected the deacons who were appointed by the Twelve.

2. Autonomy and connectedness: Paul clearly saw himself authorised to set up churches on the basis of his calling by Christ. He did not need the permission of anyone. Yet he also saw it as necessary to consult with the Jerusalem community. As it happened they accepted his policy and 'James and Cephas and John, who were recognised as pillars, offered their right hand to me as a sign of partnership' (Gals 2: 9).

3. No deference: By going to Jerusalem Paul accepted a need to be connected to the church there. But while recognising that the Jerusalem church's acceptance was important he had no hesitation in challenging Peter when the latter began to keep apart from the Gentiles: he opposed him to his face 'since he was manifestly wrong' (Gals: 2:11).

4. Dissimilarities from place to place: While the whole community was involved in the election of a replacement for Judas and the selection of the first deacons, it seems that only the leaders took part in the negotiations with Paul. Secondly, while Peter initiated the appointment of Judas' replacement, the 'pillars' of the church in Jerusalem – Peter, James and John – met with Paul, but it was James who gave the ruling at the end of the Council of Jerusalem.

5. Diversity: At the Council of Jerusalem the church faced the choice of remaining exclusively Jewish or, while retaining the gifts given by God to the Jewish people, opening the doors to those who were not Jews. They chose the latter.

Finally, we need to note that the biblical evidence we are working with is always limited. Our conclusions then are at best probable. They can rarely be certain.

How did authority develop in the church after the earliest periods? In what follows I want first to look at the period up to the nineteenth century, and secondly from then to the present.

GRADUAL PRIMACY OF ROME

The seat of power in the early church lay in Jerusalem, but it moved gradually towards Rome. This was not surprising, given that Rome was the capital of the Empire. One early example of Roman primacy is given by Henry Chadwick:

> Towards the latter part of the 1st century, Rome's presiding cleric named Clement wrote on behalf of his church to remonstrate with the Corinthian Christians who had ejected clergy without either financial or charismatic endowment in favour of a fresh lot; Clement apologised not for intervening but for not having acted sooner.[1]

In 189 AD one of the fathers of the church Irenaeus wrote: 'With (the church of Rome] because of its superior origin, all the churches must agree ... and it is in her that the faithful everywhere have maintained the apostolic tradition.'[2]

In time other centres would also grow in importance and these, like Rome, were seen as patriarchies. In 451 the Council of

---

1. John McManners, *Oxford History of Christianity*, Oxford: OUP, 1990.
2. *Against Heresies* (3:3:2).

Constantinople established Constantinople as a region or patriarchate with jurisdiction over Asia Minor and other areas. This followed the Emperor's decision in 330 to move his capital from Rome to Constantinople. Eventually five patriarchs emerged: Rome, Constantinople, Antioch, Alexandria and Jerusalem.

In the fifth century, the authority of Rome and of Constantinople gradually increased, as also did rivalry between them. In 446 Pope Leo the Great claimed that 'the care of the universal church should converge towards Peter's one seat, and nothing anywhere should be separated from its Head' and he claimed 'the full range of apostolic powers that Jesus had first bestowed on the apostle Peter' (Letter XIV). In 451 the Council of Chalcedon gave equal privileges to both Rome and Constantinople but this was rejected by the Pope.

There were many reasons for tensions between the patriarchs. One was language: Latin was spoken in the West, Greek in the East. Bilingual theologians became increasingly rare so each side understood less and less about the other. In the East they allowed liturgy in local languages and a married clergy. Both were banned by Rome. There was also a major theological difference over an addition to the creed insisted on by Rome: that the Holy Spirit descended from the Father and the Son. The East rejected this. Finally in 1054 they split: a delegation from Rome went to Constantinople and called on the Patriarch Celarius to recognise the primacy of Rome. When he refused, the papal legate excommunicated him, and Celarius excommunicated the papal legates. It was not until 1965 that the anathemas were nullified.

The split of 1054 was a major rupture in Christianity. Because of the bitterness and separation, East and West grew apart in church practice. Two consequences are important for our topic: in the East they continued with a strong stress on degrees of regional autonomy: local synods had power. In the West this did not happen to the same extent which meant that, theologically, the power of the papacy increased. Secondly, papal power was balanced to a degree by ecumenical councils. In Roman theology these are meant to be gatherings of all the bishops of the world, together with the Bishop of Rome. In practice most councils did not include all the bishops, and many did not include the pope of the time. But after 1054 the universal aspect of any ecumenical council was weakened because it did not include the Orthodox from the East. Some have argued that this has weakened the teaching authority of councils called in the Roman church. Others deny this on the grounds that Rome has the fullness of truth and the fact that the Orthodox chose to separate does not change this. Whatever about the theological arguments, any doctrine proclaimed by a Roman council is weakened in the effectiveness of its application because of the split.

Many Catholics have little awareness of the split with the East because they have little contact with Orthodox Christians.

The church suffered at least as much, if not more, from the next major split, the Reformation of the sixteenth century. It has meant that for over 400 years Christians have lived separated lives. It was only in the twentieth century that the ecumenical movement began to gather pace. The changes within the church at Vatican II were remarkable. Before the council Catholics were forbidden to attend Protestant services, so we had the extraordinary position of them standing outside at funerals of their friends and neighbours. But the *Decree on Ecumenism* at the council opened the doors, so that gradually relationships have greatly improved. In fact, there has been a huge measure of agreement among a significant number of theologians on the doctrinal issues that divided the church in the sixteenth century. This has not been translated into practical unity, however, and the Catholic Church bears some of the responsibility for this.

One of the key divides between the churches of the Reformation and the Catholic Church has been over the powers of the papacy.

INCREASING POWERS OF THE PAPACY IN THE NINETEENTH CENTURY

From the second half of the nineteenth century, the power of the papacy gradually increased. This happened in parallel with the decline of the political power of the Vatican State.

Papal infallibility

In 1870 Vatican I defined papal infallibility. It limited its use strictly to those occasions on which the Pope spoke *ex cathedra*. This is a technical term which applies when the Pope:

- Speaks about a matter of faith or morals
- Addresses the whole church
- Intends his statement to be infallible and
- Makes his intention clear.

Arguably it has only been used twice for dogmatic definitions: a) the declaration of the Immaculate Conception (that Our Lady was born without original sin) in 1854; and b) the declaration that Our Lady was assumed into heaven (1950). It is worth noting that only one of these declarations has taken place since Vatican I.

Vatican I also made a strong statement about papal authority as a whole. It said that:

- Christ founded his church on Peter
- The Pope is the successor of Peter
- The Pope has supreme power of jurisdiction over the whole church, not only in faith and morals, but also in discipline and government and
- This power extends over the church spread over the whole world.

Vatican II reaffirmed the teaching of Vatican I. Bishops acting together are infallible 'when that body exercises the supreme magisterium with the successor of Peter' (*Lumen Gentium,* henceforth *LG,* 25).

It also said that Catholics have to show a 'religious submission of mind and will' to the teaching authority of the Pope, even when he is not speaking *ex cathedra*, as for example in 'authoritative teaching' which is not infallible. The Pope's will may be known from 'the character of the documents, from his frequent repetition of the same doctrine, or from his manner of speaking' (*LG* 25).

However, there is a limit to this infallibility: it does not apply if the issue is not part of divine revelation.

The failure of collegiality
Vatican II tried to introduce two major changes that would have balanced the distribution of power between the papacy and local churches. The first was a new focus on collegiality, the idea that bishops throughout the world act together in union with the pope.

The council refers to the pope as 'head of the college of bishops'. But Vatican II left the papal-bishops relationship vague. It did not change the legal power of the bishops: in practice the pope was left with supreme authority. This was seen during the council itself when Paul VI intervened in the council on many occasions. He kept four items off the council agenda: clerical celibacy, birth control, reform of the curia (the Vatican's Civil Service) and the setting up of effective structures to implement collegiality. The right of the pope to intervene and to impose his views was not questioned. There were occasions when his proposals were not accepted by the council, and the pope did not impose his views, but if he insisted, and did so in his role as pope and not only as a bishop, the council accepted his view. Papal power was therefore seen to be legally absolute, even if on occasion it could be modified in practice.

Secondly, while the council was thinking about proposals to set up some sort of permanent international structure in Rome to implement ideas about collegiality Paul VI announced the creation of the Synod of Bishops. This was a pre-emptive strike by the papacy: the synod's powers were strictly limited. Its agenda is set by the papacy. It meets at the request of the pope. Its documents need papal approval.

Thirdly, the council had discussed the idea of returning to the practice of local synods. These had been common in the church before the split with the East. Thereafter, synods continued in the East but for the most part died out in the Roman, Western church. Informal meetings of bishops in different regions had taken place before the council, for example in Latin America. After the council these became more formalised and it is now common practice for bishops to meet in episcopal conferences in many countries.

What is the status of these local conferences? Can they issue rulings on matters of faith or morals for the Catholics of Ireland?

John Paul II's answer to this was effectively No. In 1998 he issued a ruling which stated that bishops' conferences could only issue doctrinal statements if there was unanimous agreement or if they got prior papal approval. Requiring absolute unanimity means that one negative vote can always block a proposal. Requiring prior papal approval effectively means that the conference cannot take a view different from that of the Vatican.

Instead, John Paul allowed two situations in which bishops had authority: one was the individual bishop within his diocese. The second was when bishops were gathered together in an ecumenical council.

Ladislas Orsy takes issue with this view.[1] He suggests that the Pope's position does not give sufficient attention to the fact that the bishop receives his powers at his ordination, not from the Pope, but from God. Christ promised to be with his church and to protect it from basic error. Bishops, in their role as leaders of their dioceses, share in this guarantee. Orsy argues that this applies not only when they are alone, but also when they gather together. The promise of Christ is present therefore in Bishops Conferences. The 1998 document, as Orsy sees it, confines this power of bishops.

Increased power in appointing bishops and globalisation

At the beginning of the nineteenth century the vast majority of bishops worldwide were not appointed by the Vatican. In 2012 nearly all were. That fact alone has inevitably increased the power of the papacy. It has come about for several reasons. One is that there has been an increasing separation between the church and secular powers. In the past many appointments were controlled by local princes and this was often related to financial benefits. Now that is less and less the case.

Secondly, globalisation has meant vastly increased communication. In the nineteenth century, if the Pope wanted to communicate with Archbishop McHale of Tuam in Ireland he sent an emissary to him. The Archbishop would certainly have learnt in advance of the approach of the emissary and if he did not want to meet him he simply got out of town. Now he would get an email and the Vatican would expect a fast response.

The impact of globalisation on the increase of the practical power of the papacy has not been given much attention by theologians, yet it has been critical in increasing that power.

After the council, what happened in practice was that papal power was strengthened and that of bishops reduced.

---

1. Ladislas Orsy, *Receiving The Council: Theological and Canonical Insights and Debates*, Minnesota, Liturgical Press, 2009, p. 21.

Balance between papacy and bishops

Vatican II saw collegiality as a counterbalance to the power of the papacy. This did not mean that the Bishop of Rome cannot act for the whole church independently of the bishops. But because collegiality gives authority to the bishops in union with the papacy the pope has to take account of their views.

We see the problem in that last paragraph: on the one hand the council stresses 'collegiality'. That sounds like the pope should only act together with the college of bishops. On the other hand, the pope is free to act on his own: which means that there is not a balance of power. Power remains in the hands of the papacy if the pope chooses to use it. There is a tension between the two views.

In fact there have been tensions in history between the balance of power between the papacy and ecumenical councils. During the period when the papacy was expelled from Rome to Avignon (1305-77), the fact that all the popes were French, together with 80% of the cardinals and 70% of other papal officers, led the Council of Constance (1414-1418) to depose two claimants to the papacy and to declare that councils were superior to popes. Proponents of the primacy of councils also argued that the protection against error had been given by Our Lord, through Peter and the apostles, not to the papacy, but to the whole church, and councils represented the whole church. The theory was rejected by the Fifth Lateran Council (1512-17) at which Julius II re-asserted the primacy of the papacy.

There are echoes of this dispute today over the issue of 'reception'. This is a technical term which refers to the role of the church as a whole in consenting to a teaching. The church believes that this is not a necessary condition for teaching to be irreformable. Many theologians, however, argue that universal acceptance is a confirming sign of the truth of teaching.

This suggests that to say, on the one hand, that the pope is independent of the bishops and can act without reference to them is incorrect. On the other hand, to say that councils can act without reference to the pope is incorrect. That leaves a good deal of space for other possibilities to be explored.

Both approaches were present at Vatican II. Because of this

some argue that the council was divided. But in fact the documents were accepted in all cases by an overwhelming majority of the bishops who voted on them and by Paul VI. Further, the council rejected the idea of a papacy acting without reference to the bishops of the world, because that had been proposed in the first draft of the document on the church which the bishops rejected.

However, the council set up no structures to implement their vision and it was left to the papacy to do this. Since the council, different popes have acted to strengthen the power of the papacy and weaken the power of bishops. These changes mean that whatever we have now is not the balance envisioned by the council. The council also emphasised another theme: the People of God. In doing so they wanted to give an increased role to lay people in the church.

Reduction in the power of lay people
Before the council, church teaching had stressed the hierarchy of the church: pope, bishops, priests, laity, in descending order of authority and significance. In returning to the older idea of the People of God, the council fathers meant that if we want to talk about the church we need to start with the whole People of God. They wanted all the People of God to be involved in a new way in the teaching of the church. They did not spell out in detail what this meant. But it obviously raised the question of the role of lay people. Before the council they were seen as passive recipients of church teaching. The council pointed out that all the people have an anointing which comes from God through their baptism. This ensures that they – the whole people – cannot err in matters of belief (*LG* 12). The 'sense of the faithful' of the whole people is shown when together they accept the teaching of the magisterium.

What did this mean? Many things. One was that popes, bishops and priests are not the most important people in the church: the people are. The people include all the roles within the church, ordained and non-ordained. But as people we are all equal members. Lay people are not second-class citizens. They, like popes, bishops and priests, are members of the People of God because they are baptised.

We might find this surprising if we looked at the church today: it does not look like an institution in which lay people are just as important as clerics. Yet it is the whole people who receive the promise of Christ that he will be faithful to them. It is the whole people who receive the promise of Christ that he will protect them from error. It is the whole people who are sent on a mission to bring Christ's faith, peace and justice to the world:

> The whole body of the faithful who have an anointing that comes from the Holy One (cf 1 Jn 2:20 and 27) cannot err in matters of belief. This characteristic is shown in the supernatural appreciation of the faith (*sensus fidei*) of the whole people, when 'from the bishops to the last of the faithful' they manifest a universal consent in matters of faith and morals. By this appreciation of the faith, aroused and sustained by the Spirit of truth, the People of God, guided by the sacred teaching authority (*magisterium*), and obeying it, receives not the mere word of men, but truly the word of God (cf 1 Thess 2:13), the faith once for all delivered to the saints (cf Jude 3). The people unfailingly adheres to this faith, penetrates it more deeply with right judgement, and applies it more fully in daily life (*LG* 12).

That is a dense but important statement by the council. It is worth unpacking some of the points in it:

- The Catholic church believes it is descended from the group of disciples that Jesus called together
- It believes that Jesus promised to be with these disciples in the future through the Holy Spirit who descended on them after his ascension
- In part this meant that the Spirit would protect the community from major error
- This gift is given in the first instance to all the People of God. Within the people certain groups have roles, rights and duties
- The protection of the whole church from error can be seen when the whole people show a consensus on issues of faith and morals
- Within the people the teaching authority of the church has a special role of guidance
- When the people as a whole receive the teaching of the magisterium and obey it they are receiving the word of God

As we saw above, there are tensions within these statements between the power of the people and the power of the teaching authority of the church.

The document goes on to say that this sense of the faithful is guided by the magisterium and obeys it.

That sums up the tension: on the one hand the whole people, which includes lay people, receives the anointing from God which ensures that the church cannot err. That suggests that lay people, as part of the People of God, need to be involved in the development and explanation of doctrine. This would be part of their sharing in Christ's role as prophet.

On the other hand. the laity are to obey the teaching of the magisterium which gets a special charism for teaching from God.

The council did not resolve that tension. Since the council, however, the powers of lay people have been reduced. Canon 129 of the *Code of Canon Law*, introduced in 1983, ruled that no layperson can exercise the 'power of governance' in the church. Under the previous law this was not the case. Many of the earlier councils in the church were called by lay people – including Emperors. In the case of the Council of Florence in 1452 the majority of the participants were lay. Ladislas Orsy points out that for centuries abbesses 'exercised "quasi-Episcopal jurisdiction" in governing "quasi-dioceses" – except in dispensing the sacraments, for which ordination was necessary. Such lay "prelates" had the "power of jurisdiction" – with the full and direct support of the Holy See well into the nineteenth century.'[1] As a lay man, Charles Borromeo was made a Cardinal by Pope Pius IV in 1559 at the age of twenty one.

After the council the assumption grew that lay people cannot participate in the power of the bishop. Orsy argues that: 'There is no theological reason why a bishop could not let a qualified person "participate" in his power to govern provided such participation does not encroach on the exclusive charism that is given by ordination'.[2]

The decline in practice and in canon law of the influence of laity in the church is surely the opposite of what the council fathers at Vatican II wanted.

1. Orsy, p. 39.
2. Orsy, p. 40.

This overview suggests that all is not well with our church structures. But is this issue connected with the response to the abuse crisis? I believe it is. One connection is in the style of Vatican teaching and it is to that which we now turn.

CHAPTER SEVEN

Style of Vatican Teaching

Introduction

It is clear that all is not well with Catholic church structures. The brief historical outline showed some of the changes that occurred over the centuries. Many of the values that are prominent in the Old Testament, in the life of Christ, in the early church, and in the life of the church since then seem absent today. It is therefore not surprising that John Paul II asked people for help to reform the church. The question also arises to what extent the particular structures of the church made the response to abuse more likely.

A number of charges have been made against the style of teaching that has been practised by the Vatican in the past thirty years: that it is authoritarian, sexist and homophobic. How valid are these?

Authoritarianism?

One charge is that the teaching is authoritarian, that it relies too much and too often on the powers given to the magisterium and too little on arguments it puts forward in support of teaching. An example is banning discussion of contested issues, such as the ordination of women. This is unlikely to be persuasive. It smacks of fear and fear will not help the cause of truth.

To avoid the charge the Vatican would need to show that it addresses some of the following issues in its exercise of authority:

- Does it seek consensus to the greatest extent possible?
- Does it do all it can to develop stronger consultative – and arguably more than consultative – bodies on a regional level, such as synods, bishops conferences with real power, and lay involvement? The term 'co-responsibility' is used in the Armagh diocese, for example, referring to the role of laity and clergy on the diocesan pastoral council. But can the role be 'co-responsible' if in fact it is only the bishop who has executive authority? While no one could accuse Cardinal Brady of being authoritarian, the law of the church, it seems, means that there is nothing to stop his successor being so.

- What sort of dialogue processes does the Vatican set up? Do they include only participants who already agree with its position?
- Does it appoint only like-minded bishops, or is it willing to recognise that a greater diversity within the church is appropriate, based both on the fact that historically there has been diversity on many issues, and that diversity currently exists in the church: are all the people who disagree with the Vatican on some issue always wrong?
- To what extent is its commitment to secrecy counterproductive? There is a place for confidentiality. But there is also a need for transparency. An agency made up of church outsiders as well as insiders is needed to decide the principles that should govern the balance between confidentiality and transparency and to oversee its implementation. It is not possible for an executive credibly to decide for itself what the balance should be and then to oversee it.
- Lack of accountability both in the Vatican and local dioceses was an important factor in the failure to safeguard children. Ordinary prudence and justice require oversight and accountability. This raises a doctrinal question: if the pope and local bishops have full authority in their respective areas, how can there be effective structures of accountability? Doctrinally, are we saying that Jesus wanted such a structure? Or should we be much more cautious in deciding what Our Lord wanted since the scriptural evidence is necessarily limited and interpretations of it vary so much?

Sexism?

The Vatican is accused by many of sexism. In part this is because John Paul II, echoing previous popes, declared that the church has no authority to confer priestly ordination on women because Christ did not do so, and because this has been the traditional position of the church. In a church which bases its existence on tradition – the story of the life, death and resurrection of Christ – tradition is important. The Vatican has also restricted discussion of the issue.

If the church teaches that only the ordained can exercise authority in the church, and if women cannot be ordained then the logic is that only men can exercise authority. It is difficult to avoid the charge that the end result of this is sexist.

If the church teaches that women cannot be ordained, why should it also exclude them from all exercise of authority? Since the 1983 *Code of Canon Law* lay people are excluded by canon law from all important decision-making in the church. While allowed to participate in some decision-making bodies such as parish finance committees, there is no requirement that these bodies have a lay majority. As we have seen, in the past lay people, including kings and politicians, exercised considerable power. It is also perfectly possible for a bishop or pope to delegate an element of authority. Why do the heads of Roman congregations, which effectively act as civil service departments of the Vatican, need to be ordained? Why can women not be appointed to these posts? Why also, as others have suggested, can women not be made Cardinals? A key function of Cardinals is to elect a new pope. But these functions could be extended to other governance roles in the church. Why not make a majority of the College of Cardinals women so that they can have a major influence on the appointment of the next pope?

There are examples in some countries of women being appointed as administrators of parishes, where they effectively act as parish priest, except for presiding at the Eucharist, hearing confessions and giving the Sacrament of the Sick.

In the New Testament there are examples of women in leadership roles. Phoebe, 'a deaconess of the church at Cenchreae' (Corinth), Prisca, a 'fellow-worker' of Paul's, Mary 'who worked so hard for you', Junia, an 'outstanding apostle' and Lydia are all mentioned by Paul in Romans chapter 16. Lydia traded in purple goods and after her baptism she offered hospitality in her home to Paul (Acts 16: 14-15). Euodia and Syntyche were prominent in the church in Philippi as we can see from Paul's plea to them to make peace with each other (Phil 4:2). In the view of scripture scholar Raymond Brown all this points to the prominent position played by women in the early church.

As we have seen St John in his gospel presents Mary of Magdala as being the first to whom the Risen Lord appeared, as someone who accepted and believed the good news, and who then went to announce the good news to others. In St John's theology this gives her the status of an apostle (although John does not use this term), which is why John Paul II called her the 'Apostle of the Apostles'.

However, we need to be careful about assuming that New Testament terms mean the same as they did later in the life of the church. For example, the term 'apostle' had many meanings and Paul used it to refer to those who saw the risen Christ and began to preach the gospel. Many of these must have been women. Clearly the term in the New Testament was not confined to the Twelve. Raymond Brown points out that the term cannot be used one way or the other in arguments over women's ordination as Eucharistic priests because these were still evolving at the time Paul wrote his letters. If Mary Magdalene was not ordained, as we currently understand the term, then we have both ordained and non-ordained apostles. Either way it suggests that women had authority in the early Christian community. If this is correct, we cannot argue on the basis of the New Testament that women should not exercise authority today.

Although bishops appointed in recent years seem to have been vetted on their attitudes to women's ordination some have raised questions about it. An example is Bishop Franz-Joseph of Osnabruck in Germany who said that an all-male priesthood promoted abnormalities and he called for women to be ordained deacons.[1]

We need to find a way to allow authority in the church for the non-ordained, or else to open a discussion on the ordination of women. If we do neither the charge of sexism will certainly not go away.

Homophobia?

The church is accused of discrimination against gay and lesbian people. This is a serious charge because such discrimination leads to terrible suffering, including murder and suicide. In response the church opposes discrimination: 'It is deplorable that homosexual persons have been and are the object of violent malice in speech or in action. Such treatment deserves condemnation from the church's pastors wherever it occurs.'[2] But the church

1. *The Tablet*, 31 July 2010.
2. Congregation For The Doctrine of the Faith, *Letter To The Bishops Of The Catholic Church On The Pastoral Care Of Homosexual Persons* (10).

also teaches that homosexuality and lesbianism are 'objective disorders'. Benedict XVI approved the 2005 *Instruction of the Congregation for Catholic Education* which opposed the admission of people with homosexual tendencies to ordination even if they are celibate because their condition suggests a serious personality disorder that detracts from their ability to serve as ministers:

> Bishops cannot admit to the seminary or to holy orders those who practice homosexuality, present deep-seated homosexual tendencies or support the so-called 'gay culture'.
>
> Such persons, in fact, find themselves in a situation that gravely hinders them from relating correctly to men and women. One must in no way overlook the negative consequences that can derive from the ordination of persons with deep-seated homosexual tendencies.[1]

In 1986, as Prefect of the Congregation for the Doctrine of the Faith, the then Cardinal Ratzinger oversaw the publication of the *Letter To The Bishops Of The Catholic Church On The Pastoral Care Of Homosexual Persons* which said that 'Although the particular inclination of the homosexual person is not a sin, it is a more or less strong tendency ordered toward an intrinsic moral evil; and thus the inclination itself must be seen as an objective disorder'. He re-affirmed his view in an interview with German journalist Peter Seewald in 2010:

> Homosexuality is incompatible with the priestly vocation. Otherwise, celibacy itself would lose its meaning as a renunciation. It would be extremely dangerous if celibacy became a sort of pretext for bringing people into the priesthood who don't want to get married anyway.[2]

It is difficult for gay and lesbian people to hear these views without feeling hurt because they suggest there is something wrong with their very identity. The view of the Pope is opposed by a good number of Catholic theologians who argue that homosexual relationships can be positive if the couple are

---

1. Congregation for Catholic Education, *Instruction concerning criteria for the Discernment of Vocations with regard to persons with Homosexual Tendencies in view of their admission to the Seminary and to Holy Orders*, 4 November 2005.
2. *Catholic News Service*, 24 November, 2010.

lovingly and exclusively committed to each other. Other Catholics, such as Eve Tushnet, a celibate lesbian, thinks sex is over-emphasised in discussions of homosexuality. She sees the central aspect of being gay as 'a recognition of a need for a certain kind of relationship with somebody of the same sex. That relationship need not involve sex'.[1]

Allegedly many priests are gay, but because of papal teaching they often feel the need to keep quiet about this. Most psychologists believe that, while there is a spectrum in sexual orientation, most people cannot change their orientation after adolescence. Feeling a need to hide their orientation is just as unhealthy as the need some have to proclaim it to the whole world. Further, the logic of the views of the Congregation For Catholic Education would seem to call for the resignation from the priesthood of those who are gay. This would mean a loss to the church of many gifted priests.

The reality is that there are different voices on the issue of homosexuality within the church. Vincent Nichols, Archbishop of Westminster, admitted that: 'When it comes to understanding what human sexuality is for, there is a lot that we have to explore.' When asked if the church would one day accept gay unions he said: 'I don't know. Who knows what's down the road?'[2] The Vatican's insistence that its view is the only correct one and its relying on the authority of the magisterium to reinforce this will not make the divisions go away. Those who agree with the Vatican will be pleased, those who are opposed are unlikely to be persuaded.

Given the Vatican's view it is particularly important that great care is taken within the church to ensure that there is no discrimination in practice against gay and lesbian people. As with all discrimination, it is crucial that the group who are threatened play a central role in ascertaining whether such discrimination exists or not. It is important, then, for the church to ensure that a reasonable proportion of gay and lesbian people are represented on different church bodies. This means introducing into the church some of the proofing for diversity tests that are applied in secular society.

1. Eve Tushnet, 'On Faith', *The Washington Post*, 23 November 2010.
2. *The Tablet*, 8 January 2011, p. 33.

Teaching authority and disagreement

What happens when there is no consensus in the church, when, for example, a large proportion of the People of God do not accept the teaching of the magisterium? The dispute over birth control is an example: many of the People of God do not accept the teaching of *Humanae Vitae* that the use of artificial birth control is wrong in all circumstances.

One response is to say that the people who reject the teaching are clearly wrong: it is the magisterium that teaches. It has spoken. It is the duty of the people to obey.

For that view to be in harmony with Vatican II we would need to delete the statement in *LG* 12 that: 'The entire body of the faithful, anointed as they are by the Holy One, (111) cannot err in matters of belief' and that they show this special characteristic when there is consensus between bishops and laity. Instead the council should have said something like: 'The anointing of the Holy One means that the whole church cannot err. And this is shown when the magisterium teaches and the rest of the people accept it.' That would suggest that the gift of being protected from error is given to the magisterium. But that is not what the council said. Rather it says that the gift is given to the whole people, and a special charism is given to the magisterium. The whole people must therefore play some role in showing that the church is protected from error, and in teasing out church teaching.

To suggest simply that all that is needed is to get people to obey the magisterium is not the teaching of Vatican II.

On the other hand it would also be incorrect to say that the magisterium is wrong because a significant number of people reject its teaching. To take that position would mean that the role of the magisterium is simply to reflect popular opinion, which would make church teaching subject to the latest cultural or popular fads. To do so would also be against council teaching. It would mean deleting all mention of the magisterium in *LG* 12. It would mean that some of the great doctrines of the church, for example, the teaching that Jesus Christ is both fully human and fully divine, was wrong because at the time it was passed it was not accepted by the majority. The wider church received it only gradually.

Clearly the last paragraph reveals a tension between the role of the People as a whole receiving a teaching of the magisterium and the role of the magisterium in developing teaching, a tension which, as discussed, existed during Vatican II.

What is needed is not a simplistic way to remove this tension but rather mechanisms to recognise and value the tension.

In the case of *Humanae Vitae* the advisory body set up by Paul VI recommended a change in teaching to allow the use of artificial contraception in some circumstances. Karol Wotyla, the future John Paul II was a member of the commission. This advice was eventually rejected by Paul VI. One motive alleged for this was his fear that making the change would show a discontinuity in papal teaching and that this would undermine papal authority.

If the allegation is correct it backfired: arguably the response to *Humanae Vitae* has done much to undermine papal authority. A consequential argument is used by many to support the encyclical: the collapse of family values has led to chaos and suffering for many. However one assesses that view, it does not touch the centre of the encyclical which teaches that the use of artificial contraception in all circumstances is objectively gravely wrong. It seems as if the teaching has been rejected by many who remain within the church. There remains therefore a question of how the church can convince the faithful of the truth of the teaching.

Dealing with allegations of heresy
Part of the responsibility of the Bishop of Rome is to proclaim God's word as revealed in scripture and tradition. Others, however, have duties also in this area, among them theologians. It is their task to seek to understand scripture and tradition, to explain church teaching that is irreformable, to probe questions that are not settled, and to articulate criteria for knowing the difference between the two.

The increased centralising of the papacy in the past 100 years has led to a parallel increase in its attempt to control dissent. That is part of the role of governance in the church: to decide what is or is not acceptable teaching. Recent Popes have been accused of imposing a narrow set of thinking on the church: this charge was made against John Paul II because, allegedly, the bishops he appointed had to show their acceptance of Vatican teaching on sex and the ordination of women.

How should the Vatican respond when it has problems with the content of theologians' teaching?

First there is nothing wrong of itself in having a degree of tension between the papacy and theologians. There will be occasions when the teaching authority will not agree with the judgments of individual theologians. There is a difference of emphasis in the two roles: the Vatican needs to preserve the tradition. Theologians need to explore it. That means probing, questioning, challenging. Secondly, there is a need for a process to decide when the boundaries of the tension have been exceeded. The Vatican has a process in place for doing this. In this respect it is no different from any other church. Unfortunately the process is a bad one. It is bad because it does not respect persons. That in itself means it operates against scriptural values. But it also means that it is less likely to discover and to cherish the truth.

Some of the bad elements of the process, highlighted by Ladislas Orsy, are:

- If theologians are suspected of false teaching in the church an investigation of their work is started by the Congregation for the Doctrine of Faith. But the persons concerned are not told of this investigation until it is well advanced. Indeed people questioned about the views of the theologians are sworn to secrecy.
- As part of the process the Congregation appoints someone to act on behalf of the suspected author. But this person is chosen by the Congregation, not by the author – who does not at this stage even know that he or she is being investigated.
- The Congregation can find the writings defective on the basis of criteria much wider than those for the denial of an article of faith. So the writing could be found to be against 'definitive teaching' by a Pope, or even against official pronouncements not intended to be definitive.
- Only at this stage is the author informed. At this point, with the consent of his or her bishop the author may choose to appoint an advisor. He or she is given three months to prepare a response. (Most theologians have a busy schedule of lectures, meetings and writing. To prepare a response at such short notice is often difficult.)

- The author has no right to appear before the Congregation but the Prefect may give permission for a dialogue to take place between the author and delegates of the Congregation.
- The Congregation then decides if the author is guilty or not. If the Pope ratifies this decision the author is given three months to correct his or her opinions. He or she may ask for permission to make a written submission. If the author has not corrected his or her views and is found guilty of heresy he or she is excommunicated. No appeal is permitted.

This process would not stand up to scrutiny in a secular legal process governed by Human Rights declarations of the UN or the EU: it shows no respect for the individual concerned. It does not show the accused details of the accusation or the material which the prosecution will use at the trial, as would be the case in a proper secular process; the initial investigation is carried out by a process including a spokesperson for the accused appointed by the Congregation, not by the accused; there is no right of appeal.[1]

The 1990 Instruction *On the Ecclesial Vocation of the Theologian*, issued by the Congregation for the Defence of the Faith, considers the complex relationship between theologians and the teaching authority of the church. It recognises that theologians on occasion may find themselves disagreeing with some teaching. If so they must make known their objections to the magisterium. This, however, must be done in private. One of the concerns of the document is that the People of God will 'not be disturbed by a particular dangerous opinion (37)'.

The judgment of the magisterium against a theologian:

[I]s the result of a thorough investigation conducted according to established procedures which afford the interested party the opportunity to clear up possible misunderstandings of his thought (37).
If it happens that the (theologians) encounter difficulties due to the character of their research, they should seek their solution in trustful dialogue with the Pastors, in the spirit of truth and charity which is that of the communion of the church (40)'.

---

1. Orsy, pp 91-104.

A key issue underlying the Instruction is the fear of relativism. That is a legitimate fear. The response to this, however, is less than adequate. The document concedes that procedures can be improved, but this 'does not mean that they are contrary to justice and right'. This is because judgments made do 'not concern the person of the theologian but the intellectual positions which he has publicly espoused'.

That may be correct about the judgement of the theologian's views. It is not correct about the procedures that lead to the judgment: these very much concern the person of the theologian and they do not treat him or her with respect. There are two consequences: one is that the human rights of the theologian are not respected. This is not because the teaching authority has disagreed with him or her – this is of course one of the functions of a teaching authority – but because the methods used to establish the views of the theologian are not respectful. The second consequence follows from the first: because the procedures are not respectful they are less likely to arrive at the truth.

There will always be differences of opinion within the church and therefore between theologians and the teaching authority. As the 1990 document says, 'The pastoral task of the magisterium is one of vigilance. It seeks to ensure that the People of God remain in the truth which sets free (20)'. But it goes on immediately to admit that this is 'a complex and diversified reality'.

This survey suggests that there is much that is wrong with the way authority is exercised within our church. There is a need for a teaching authority. But it is wrong to argue that this should involve rulers who teach and the rest who obey. Such a view does not take seriously the notion of the People of God. Saying this, however, does not answer the question of how to handle differences within the church. We need diversity, but how much?

SECTION FOUR

A Way Forward?

CHAPTER EIGHT

How much Diversity?

How much diversity can we tolerate within the church? The diversity exists: Catholics disagree on many issues, irrespective of what the Vatican says. Further, it is not clear what the Vatican achieves by repressing dissent: it certainly makes an impact on theologians who are forced to find jobs in non-Catholic controlled institutions or to keep their views to themselves, unless they accept papal rulings against its work. But does the Vatican's approach convince more people to accept its view? I doubt it. Calling for people to accept teaching on the basis of authority is always likely to be less convincing than trying to persuade them that the teaching is true.

There are individuals who can make attractive presentations in the media of false or incomplete teaching. But that problem can arguably be dealt with more effectively by looking for ways to challenge them in the media and, secondly, following the example of Gamaliel in the Acts of the Apostles, by letting time pass to see whether their teaching will survive and be shown to be 'of God' (Acts 5: 33 ff) or not.

This is not to deny the need for the magisterium to make decisions on occasion about what is of faith and what is not. We shall see shortly that many Protestant churches have shown in ecumenical dialogues that they appreciate the need for a teaching authority. But a number of criteria should be used when dealing with disputed issues:

- We need to be more cautious about disputed issues than about those about which there is universal agreement in the church.
- Theologians need to probe an issue in depth before the magisterium make any decision. Without this we are simply failing to use the tools available to us to find the truth.
- We need to be careful in deciding which truths are essential for our faith, and which are open to legitimately-held differences. Vatican II recognised a 'hierarchy of truths'. With this in mind we should ask: how high in that hierarchy is

the teaching in question? Is the teaching essential to the faith or is it one about which people may legitimately disagree?

- We need to be more cautious about decisions which increase divisions between ourselves and other Christian churches, firstly because we are called by Christ to work for unity and that means doing all we can to reduce divisions. Secondly, we need to ask why other churches take a different view and be open to learning from them, because they have many of the marks of the true church, as was recognised by Vatican II.

In the end we need to find a way to live with difference. We are unlikely to get consensus within the church in the foreseeable future on issues such as the ordination of women or gay or lesbian people, divorce and remarriage, contraception, the authority of the Vatican and other institutions in the church, liturgical questions, and a whole raft of other issues. At the moment the magisterium imposes – and the word is used deliberately – its view on all these issues. But many Catholics persist in taking a contrary position. In the view of the Vatican this means that they are not in full communion with the church. In the view of the dissidents they remain in full communion and they refuse to hand the church over to the Vatican. This often seems like a dead-end argument where the Vatican issues declarations. Those who supported these positions before the declarations are delighted. Those who opposed them continue to do so. And nothing changes. Is there a better way forward? We may have something to learn from efforts to overcome, or at least to deal with, differences in the political field.

In Northern Ireland the 'Troubles', as the conflict was euphemistically called, lasted over 30 years in its latest phase. Terrible murders were carried out by groups from all sides, including state forces. Lies and propaganda were propagated. The population was deeply divided. Yet in 2010 there was a power-sharing government in Northern Ireland made up of the most divided groups.

Not that everything was rosy: on the contrary the level of segregation in 2010 was greater than in 1998, the year of the multi-party Agreement. Nonetheless the vast majority of people had found a way to live together without killing each other. How did this happen?

There were many factors in the peace process and each was important. One element was dialogue. The word can mean many things. Here it refers to people coming together, not to agree or to negotiate, but to understand. In fact one of the ground rules for this form of dialogue was to ban agreement! Doing this removed a fear among participants that they were being asked to compromise, or that by taking part in the dialogue they were already weakening their position.

It took many hours for them to realise that they were not being asked to change their beliefs. Instead they were being asked to say what really mattered to them, and much more importantly, why it mattered to them. The normal answer to this question at first was a series of philosophical or political arguments. But gradually these changed to something else: a story. That story was about their experience in the past. It often involved pain and suffering. As they told their stories, and as they heard the stories of those whose loved ones in many cases they had killed, they gradually came to an understanding. That understanding was an insight into both their own pain and that of their opponents. The outcome was not agreement. But it did change things. Now they knew, and could tell others within their own group, why the others did what they did. Further, what the others did turned out not to be so crazy after all. Indeed, had they been in the position of the others they might have done the same thing – although everything the others did was still wrong.

These dialogues were part of a political process. Can they have any relevance in disagreements about faith truths? The initial answer may be a resounding No. Why? Because the Troubles were about politics, faith is about beliefs. In fact this is very simplistic. The Troubles were about all sorts of things and deeply-held beliefs were part of them. Further, in the dialogue most people did not change their beliefs. They did change their understanding of the other side and their understanding of why the others believed what they did.

A second, striking modern example of unity in diversity is the European Community. Its 27 member states have widely diverse legal systems, religions, values, and languages. Many have histories in which they were bitterly opposed to each other: hundreds of thousands were killed in the three major wars between France and Germany in 1870, 1914 and 1939. Many of the member states are made up of significant minority groups. Yet all the members are part of a community in which they accept the laws of the community, share political power and distribute financial and other goods.

The beliefs that matter to us in the church have not come from nowhere. They are based in part on our experiences. My appreciation of the Eucharist was helped by several events that I can recall. One was sitting on the crossbar of my father's bike as he brought me to Mass, probably when I was about seven years old. A second was looking up at my mother as a child and watching her pray at Mass. A third was when I was asked by an Anglican on my first morning at the Irish School of Ecumenics if I would give him communion. My answer was an immediate No. When asked Why? I responded that they did not believe what we believed. But he then asked me what we believed. At that point panic emerged in me as I tried desperately to remember what it was that we believed about the Eucharist! Although I already had a degree in theology I had a long way to go to internalise and probe my own Eucharistic theology. Later I learnt much from my Protestant friends in Northern Ireland through dialogue about faith and politics in the conflict. One key element of this was the theme of the covenant community in the Old Testament, and its social and political implications. A second was that of *anamnesis*, a Greek word meaning remembering, which opened up to me a greater understanding of how Jews remembered the past, and therefore of what Jesus might have meant when he used the term at the institution of the Eucharist: 'Do this in remembrance of me' (Luke 22:19).

These are only a few examples from my own life. But if we probed the experience that Christians throughout the world have of the Eucharist, or of prayer, or of listening to the Word, or of service, or of other important elements in their Christian lives, we would not, I suspect, arrive at much agreement, but we would learn a lot and our faith would be deepened. We would also find a better and more respectful way to handle our differences, even though we would still be left with hard choices which might mean some staying and some leaving the church.

There are different models of teaching. One is that the teacher has the truth and tells the students about it. They then accept it and have learnt something. The model works well in many instances: why should a three-year old not put his hand in the fire? 'Because you will get burnt. Because I told you not to do so.' The parent knows something that the child does not. The same can apply in some adult teaching: if I want to learn some science I will need to find someone who knows more about it than I do.

But the model is a bad one in conflict situations. If we follow it each side is closed to learning from the other. What then, if I want you to learn the truth? I will achieve nothing by shouting at you. On the other hand I may achieve a lot by dialogue. But if I want to dialogue with you I have to be open not only to offering you something, but also to learning something from you. Otherwise neither of us will learn anything.

While, therefore, there is a need for a teaching authority in the church, and one that at times has to make decisions based on what constitutes authentic teaching, there is also a need for dialogue as a way to advance the truth.

Ecumenical comments on the powers of bishops and laity
John Paul II explicitly included members of other churches when he looked for people to offer him critical advice on how the church should be reformed.

There has been a great development in theological understanding between the Roman Catholic and other churches since the Les Dombes meeting in France in 1937. One recent example is the Anglican-Roman Catholic document *The Gift of Authority* published in 1999. It was referred to positively by Pope Benedict XVI and the Archbishop of Canterbury, Rowan Williams, at their meeting in the Vatican on 23 November 2006.[1]

The document is not an official one of either church but it has considerable status, given that the Commission was officially appointed by both churches, and given also the positive reference to it by the Pope and Archbishop.

---

1. Pope Benedict XVI, *Address of his Holiness Benedict XVI to the Archbishop of Canterbury His Grace Rowan Williams*, 23 November 2006.

The document accepts the need for a universal primacy. This is a significant step for Anglicans. But they have in mind a primacy different in important respects from the current Roman Catholic model.

Among the points made are:

- The laity, on the basis of their baptism, play an 'integral role' in decision making.
- There should be complementarity between the papacy and the college of bishops throughout the world.
- There is a need to respect the role of local bishops, as well as that of ecumenical councils and the papacy.
- Leaders in the church 'must not be separated from the 'symphony' of the whole people of God in which they have their part to play. They need to be alert to the *sensus fidelium*' (30).
- On gatherings of local bishops: bishops' communion with each other is expressed in different ways, including local synods and councils. 'The maintenance of communion requires that at every level there is a capacity to take decisions appropriate to that level (37).' This is also a principle of Catholic Social Teaching.
- The document has a carefully nuanced statement which accepts papal infallibility in limited circumstances, as the Catholic church teaches. Every such pronouncement is seen as expressing 'only the faith of the church'. It is pronounced within the college of bishops – so the Pope is not seen as acting in some way separate from the other bishops.

The document noted the gradual strengthening within the Catholic church of episcopal conferences and canon law's requirement that lay people, religious, deacons and priests participate in parish and diocesan councils This helped the church move closer to Anglicanism. However the document also questioned whether the teaching of Vatican II on collegiality or the role of local bishops has been implemented sufficiently, and if there is sufficient consultation between Rome and local churches before making important decisions which affect the whole church.

The thrust of the document seems close to the majority view at Vatican II and less close to what has happened within the

Catholic Church since. If true, that is a serious charge. It means that the documents of the council which were approved by the bishops of at least the Western, Latin church and which were subsequently approved by the Pope have not been implemented.

This again highlights the tension in the church's teaching about the respective powers of Pope and bishops. As we have seen, arguably the wishes of the council that greater powers be given to local bishops conferences and to lay people have not been fulfilled. But, is it not the case that it is up to the Pope to decide how to implement the council? There is clearly a tension here between the status of documents which have been solemnly approved by the Pope and bishops in the council and the powers of a Pope to implement, change or ignore them subsequently. In practice it seems as if the Papacy has taken on this power in an unbalanced way since the council and that it has been allowed to do so by the bishops.

Several questions arise in the light of this. Do Popes have the authority not to implement the wishes of councils when these have been approved by the Pope and the bishops? If not, what oversight structures are in place to raise questions about whether or not the council documents have been implemented? To whom is the Pope accountable? Or is it the case that Catholic teaching endorses a fully monarchical model of the papacy, unimpeded by any structures?

The issue of diversity raises questions about the way in which different parts of the Body of Christ feed into decision-making structures. But before asking what changes in these structures might be desirable we need to face another question: did the particular structures of the church make it more likely that the response to the abuse crisis would be so awful? Or was the crisis uninfluenced by these structures?

CHAPTER NINE

What does the abuse crisis say about church structures?

It would be wrong to argue that inadequacies in church structures were the cause of either clerical child abuse or the appalling
response to it. Abuse and poor responses to it have happened in
many different contexts, including in other churches, in secular
institutions, and in wider society. However, it may still be true
that poor structures, and the values that they embodied made it
more likely that the abuse took place in the first place or that the
response to it was so poor.

Why did the abuse happen?
There were many reasons but the following seem particularly
important:

1. The church and the society of the time were patriarchal or
    male dominated.
2. The perceived superiority of clergy and religious.
3. Church authorities were not accountable to external agencies.
4. There was a culture of deference towards clergy and religious.
5. Church systems were not transparent and so could operate
    with secrecy.

A patriarchal church and society
A patriarchal society is one dominated by males. This does not
mean that women are without power, but that the power they
have is usually dependent on colluding in male power or manipulation. This is not because women are any more biased towards manipulation than males – they are not – but because
manipulation is one of the few weapons available to the less
powerful in society.

Ireland up to quite recently was a highly-patriarchal society, and
serious symptoms of patriarchy are still visible, for example, in low
representation of women in parliaments and in the male domination
of higher posts in the public and private sector. But it was much
worse in the past.

A mark of a patriarchal society is that it favours men's sexual demands. So in the past marital rape was not seen as a crime. Domestic violence was seen as a matter internal to families. Many church leaders and members saw abuse as something internal to the church.

Unaccountable power, lack of transparency, the perception of superiority, secrecy so as to protect the powerful from scandal and deference are features of a patriarchal society.

The church has many marks of patriarchy. The role of women in the church and their exclusion from any executive role within the church is one example.

Deference and the perceived superiority of clergy and religious

The culture in Ireland up to about 1970 saw celibacy as superior to marriage and this was supported with theological arguments. The culture in this instance may well have been influenced by economic arguments. Landowners in post-famine Ireland could not divide their property between their children without destroying its economic viability: the plots would have been too small to support a family. One response was emigration to the UK, US and other areas. A second was to ensure that only the eldest son inherited the land. A third was to encourage young people to think of the priesthood or religious life, which were both celibate. In the theology and culture of the time this meant young people giving themselves to God by devoting themselves to God's work: lay people who lived in the world could also serve God, but not in as high a way.

The Famine ended in 1847, but Ireland remained a poor country, despite political independence, up to the 1980s. The gap between rich and poor was large, and many were very poor.

In this culture, and helped by some theological thinking in the church before Vatican II, clergy and religious were put on a pedestal. Most people rightly reject this today in Ireland. It is a feature of all clerical societies. It can still be seen in other countries where there is a great gap between rich and poor and the society is heavily patriarchal. In this context religion can help people deal with the awfulness of life. Clergy are seen as representatives of religion and so they are put on a pedestal. This is a disaster for clergy, people and the gospel, and also for child protection within the church.

An unintended consequence of the definition of papal infallibility was that it almost certainly added to the idea that priests and religious were superior. While this has nothing to do with the doctrine, there is an easily-made jump from belonging to an institution which sees itself as infallible – no matter how technical and restricted the actual dogma is – to seeing the officers of the institution as superior beings.

The Murphy Report in Ireland mentioned deference as a key element that made abuse more likely. The perceived superiority of clergy and religious was key to this: people often felt they should not challenge a priest or religious: they were men or women 'of God'. Abusers quite explicitly used their status to achieve their ends. Superiors and bishops protected their men and sometimes their women in order to protect the name of the church: exposing them would have led to 'scandal'. The laity would have been shocked. The name of the church would have been besmirched. And so the abusers were protected. The scandal in the end, of course, was all the more grave.

Many blame celibacy for the crisis. Yet the rate of abuse in other churches with married clergy is comparable to that of the Catholic Church. In the wider society a very high proportion of abuse is carried out within the family. This can be by siblings who are not married, but much of it is also by fathers, step-fathers, grandfathers and uncles. I know of no evidence suggesting that celibates are more likely to abuse than sexually active people.

In Ireland many thousands of young people joined the priesthood and religious life, often at a very early age. They therefore had no preparation for a life of celibacy. But once they had joined it was not easy for them to leave: doing so brought the stigma of the 'spoiled' priest or religious. They also did not want to let parents down. They received little training in sexuality and such training as they did receive often focused on the evils of sexual sins. That tended towards a guilt-ridden spirituality. The combination of joining young, poor sexual education, and guilt, probably made abuse more likely.

However, the issue raised by this is not celibacy as such, but rather allowing people to join a religious order or the priesthood at too early an age without adequate sexual maturity.

This, combined with a spirituality that promoted guilt and secrecy about sexuality and the fact that many were abused by others who themselves had joined at too early an age, made abuse more likely.

Within this combination of factors celibacy played an indirect role: it was used as one of the ways to show that the clerical and religious life was superior. In that way it contributed indirectly to the problem. If celibacy itself was at the centre of the problem one would expect abuse rates to be much higher among clerics than married people and that does not seem to be the case. The vast majority of abuse is carried out in families. One would also expect to see lower abuse rates in other churches in which clergy are married. Again this seems not to be the case.

Deference and perceived superiority is at the heart of clericalism. This is not simply a thing of the past. In 2011 Bishop Tom Burns warned: 'that clericalism risks raising its head today among those who again are looking for identity in status, not service ... Some want to put the priest on a pedestal, while the people are consigned to be privileged spectators outside the rails. Flamboyant modes of liturgical vestments and rubrical gestures abound. Women are denied all ministries at Mass ... To many in our church and beyond, this comes across as triumphalism and male domination.'[1]

Lack of accountability
If there is one factor that stands out above all others it is that the power of popes, bishops, priests and religious was too often unaccountable. Such accountability as existed was vertical, not horizontal. So a priest or religious could be held accountable to his superior or bishop. The bishop or superior might have to give occasional reports to their respective line managers, but reporting requirements were limited – bishops have to give a report on their ministry to Rome only every five years.

Lack of transparency
Bishops and superiors have a special relationship with those under their authority. Some, for example, Cardinal Castrillon Hoyos, head of the Vatican's Congregation for the Clergy, as

---

1. 'Bishop warns of clericalism behind sex abuse', *The Tablet*, 8 January 2011.

already mentioned, saw the bishop-priest relationship as analogous to that of parents with their children. There are parallels with the difficulties any family would have in reporting one of its members to the police. Bishops and superiors had a duty of confidentiality, similar in some respects to that of lawyers or of journalists. There was also the question of establishing the truth: should the bishop or superior believe the accused or not? It is well known that those who abuse can be extremely manipulating and convincing.

Confidentiality is a value in society. But there are other values which conflict with it, such as being publicly accountable. In the culture of the time, greater weight was given to confidentiality in cases of religious and clerics than those involving lay people: the latter were often reported to the police. They did not have the same confidential relationship with bishops and superiors.

Why did good bishops and superiors respond so badly?
Some of the bishops and superiors who dealt with clerical and religious abusers were outstanding leaders: it was precisely because of this that they were appointed to their positions. It is dangerous to explain their actions on the grounds that they were ogres: doing so does not help us to understand why they did what they did and so does not help us to prevent similar occurrences in the future. Many saw themselves and were seen by those who knew them well as being highly committed to gospel values, including defence of the most vulnerable. The key question, then, is how did they get it so wrong and end up allowing abuse to continue for so long, with devastating results for the children involved? Why did they not go to the police? Why did they continue to move people from one situation to another where abuse continued?

Understanding, of course why people acted as they did, does not excuse, minimise or justify the harm done.

As we have seen, there was quite limited knowledge about the dynamics of child abuse even among professionals up to about 1980 and bishops and superiors, like others, needed to go through a learning curve. This was one reason why people acted as they did. This explanation does not apply to later actions when the dynamics of abuse were understood better.

Most of us would like to think that had we been in a position of authority we would have acted differently. The wrong done by the response to the abuse is so obvious that it is hard to believe how anyone acted as the leaders did.

In fact the assumption that the rest of us would have responded differently is dangerous. Regrettably, the findings of many studies in social psychology suggest that our communal capacity for acting badly is far greater than most of us realise or would like to admit. The Milgram experiments in the US in 1963 showed that over 60 per cent of people were willing to electrocute an innocent person in response to an order, albeit in a simulated experiment (although the participants thought that they were killing the person who was acting as a student).[1]

Philip Zimbardo's 1971 Stanford prison experiment[2] showed how fast people can get out of control when they are in a position of unaccountable power. Zimbardo names seven factors that are likely to 'grease the slippery slope to evil'. Two of these are blind obedience to authority and uncritical conformity to group norms.[3]

Both were – and are – grave dangers within the Catholic Church. When the tendency of people to obey authority is linked to authority given by God and when people are working for an institution which is seen as part of the expression of the presence of Christ in the world, the dangers of uncritical obedience are greatly increased. This comment is not an argument against authority in general or in the church: authority is needed in any case, and there are scriptural arguments for church authority. But if obedience can be a virtue, it can also be a source of

1. Milgram tested the extent to which volunteer participants would obey orders even when these conflicted with their morals. Participants were asked to administer what they thought was an electric shock of increasing degrees to a student every time he gave an incorrect answer to a question. The 'student' was an actor who mimed responses to the apparent shock. 65% of participants delivered the maximum shock which was labelled 'XXX'. The previous level was labelled 'danger: severe shock'.
2. In the Stanford prison experiment researchers set up a mock prison and then selected 24 students to play the roles of both prisoners and guards. Prisoners remained in the mock prison 24 hours a day. Guards were allowed to return home after an eight hour shift. The experiment had to be stopped after just six days instead of the planned fourteen because the guards became abusive and prisoners began to show signs of stress and anxiety.
3. www.ted.com, *What Makes People Go Wrong*, Filmed in 2008.

evil and crime. The less accountable and transparent authority is and the more it is influenced by a patriarchal culture the more likely obedience will tend towards evil.

Towards the beginning of Mark's gospel we are told the story of Jesus curing Simon Peter's mother-in-law. When she was cured she got up and ministered to them (Mk 1:29 ff). It is a beautiful passage which goes on to recount how all the people brought their sick to the house and were cured. Yet it also reveals a patriarchal society: it was Peter's mother-in-law who prepared the meal, not one of the men because in that society clear roles were assigned to and accepted by women. The disciples – and Jesus himself – were part of that system of patriarchy because they were men of their time and their culture. That should help us to understand how good people can be part of – and contribute to – bad systems.

Structures and the response to abuse

This survey suggests that there was a connection between the type of structures we have in the church and the response to abuse. The major reasons for the failure to respond properly were:

- Patriarchy,
- The perceived superiority of clergy and religious,
- The fact that church authorities were not accountable to external agencies,
- Deference to clergy and religious,
- The lack of transparency, and,
- Up to the early 1980s, limited knowledge of the issue among professionals.

Understanding the influence of systems should encourage us to be more open to questioning our culture and our structures. In the church the papacy has supreme authority. As we have seen this has grown since the nineteenth century. What are the consequences of such a centralised authority?

CHAPTER TEN

Consequences of the Increase in Papal Power

The power of the papacy has increased at a practical and arguably at a doctrinal level since Vatican II. The documents of
Vatican II show some compromises which, if followed through,
would have led to a more effective balance of power between
the papacy and bishops. It would also have led to lay people
being consulted to a greater extent, but still having no executive
function.

What are the consequences of this?
One is doctrinal: in Catholic teaching the papal office has been
given certain powers. It seems that among these is the power to
determine the extent of the powers of the office. In other words,
if some theologians or others in the church question whether the
papacy has certain powers, the papacy itself has the power to
decide the answer. Similarly, if a council consisting of the Pope
and bishops meeting together decides on changes in the balance
of power between the papacy and bishops, the papacy has the
power to decide if and how these should be implemented.

Given this, given also that the papacy now appoints nearly
all bishops and can ensure that their thinking is in accordance
with Vatican values, and given the increased means of communication which help to ensure that they remain on message, the
power of the Vatican in internal church control is greater within
the church than at any time in history.

There are of course limitations to papal power: the Pope can
only teach what is already present in revelation or necessary to
protect it. Teaching on faith or morals has to be consistent with
respect for persons and in accordance with the natural law.

Arguably, there is one advantage in having a strong, centralised papacy. As the abuse crisis unfolded, countries not affected
by it looked at those that were. They were staggered at the levels
of crime and thanked God that nothing like that could happen in
their situation. I was guilty of this myself as I looked at the crisis
unfolding in the US. But of course it turned out that the Irish
church was more than capable of similar crimes. These crimes

can happen anywhere. But they are particularly likely to happen in contexts where there is a) unaccountable power; b) deference to clergy; c) a patriarchal society; d) large gaps between rich and poor.

There are many countries around the world in which the Catholic Church is strong in which each of these conditions is met. Only a strong, centralised and pro-active papacy can take effective action to set in place proper child-protection structures and to expose crimes from the past. Not only do structures need to be in place, but these need to include oversight. If we have learnt anything from the abuse crisis we know that these structures need to be independent.

Only a strong papacy with a proper theological basis for its powers, a new canon law based on these values, and an effective bureaucracy, can enforce the changes needed. I use the word 'enforce' deliberately because we know the pattern of denial, avoidance and secrecy that each country in turn has gone through on this issue. A new structure to deal with the issue needs to have the power to overrule bishops within their own diocese. In the current Catholic theology of bishops only a structure with the full sanction of the papacy can do this.

Many also see advantages in a stronger, more centralised papacy for doctrinal reasons. In a post-modernist world in which opposing views are seen as having equal value, a strong papacy can insist that Catholic teaching takes a clear line on disputed issues, for example the ordination of women or gay or lesbian people. It is because they see the Catholic Church as being true to the tradition that a considerable number of Anglicans have left their own communion to join the Roman church.

However, there are also disadvantages to a centralised papacy which need to be considered.

One is that the papacy developed the style of a monarch. In part this was because popes often were absolute rulers of the Vatican State. But it was also because they claimed and were often given supreme ecclesiastical jurisdiction. Given Catholic doctrine and practice, it is almost impossible for a pope not to be given the trappings of a monarch, no matter how much he may dislike this. The trappings which go with a monarchical papacy are deeply opposed to the values and example of Christ as revealed in the gospels. They have also increased the mystique surrounding the person of the pope. Bishop Kevin Dowling argues:

> What compounds this, for me, is the mystique which has in increasing measure surrounded the person of the pope in the last thirty years, such that any hint of critique or questioning of his policies, his way of thinking, his exercise of authority etc is equated with disloyalty. There is more than a perception, because of this mystique, that unquestioning obedience by the faithful to the pope is required and is a sign of the ethos and fidelity of a true Catholic. When the pope's authority is then intentionally extended to the Vatican curia, there exists a real possibility that unquestioning obedience to very human decisions about a whole range of issues by the curial departments and cardinals also becomes a mark of one's fidelity as a Catholic, and anything less is interpreted as being disloyal to the pope who is charged with steering the barque of Peter.
>
> It has become more and more difficult over the past years, therefore, for the college of bishops as a whole, or in a particular territory, to exercise their theologically-based servant leadership to discern appropriate responses to their particular socio-economic, cultural, liturgical, spiritual and other pastoral realities and needs; much less to disagree with or seek alternatives to policies and decisions taken in Rome.[1]

Secondly, giving great power to an individual or institution is dangerous. We need to be mindful of Acton's aphorism: 'Power tends to corrupt, and absolute power corrupts absolutely.'[2]

Thirdly, I have argued that a key issue behind clerical abuse was unaccountable power. Increasing the power of the papacy, as the church has done since the middle of the nineteenth century, including, for example, the power to decide how council decrees are implemented, inevitably creates a context of unaccountable power. That is dangerous.

Fourthly, an increasingly centralised papacy can lose the energy, enthusiasm and commitment of local regions and dioceses.

---

1. Kevin Dowling, 'South Africa: Bishop Dowling reflects on Trends in the Church', *Independent Catholic News*, 8 July 2010.
2. John Emerich Edward Dalberg-Acton, *Essays on Freedom and Power*, Boston: Beacon Press, 1949, p. 364.

Fifthly, many lay people will not be attracted to local diocesan councils if these are confined to a purely advisory role and if they have no real influence on the teaching and practice of the church.

Sixthly, an over-strong papacy is more likely to put the church above internal criticism. One could theoretically argue that it is possible to accept the monarchical model and engage in robust criticism. But this is unlikely. The more obvious outcome is what existed at the end of the millennium: great deference to the papacy. It is unlikely to lead to exchanges like, for example, those between Peter and Paul in the New Testament. Deference was one of the elements which led to the poor response to abuse.

Seventhly, a monarchical papacy without proper accountability does not have sufficient protection from the dangers of falling into human rights abuses. Some of the treatment of theologians is an example of this.

Eighthly, the concentration of authority in the centre contradicts one of the tenets of Catholic social teaching, subsidiarity; which holds that all things that can be done at a lower level of society should not be taken over by a higher level.

A ninth disadvantage is that a monarchical papacy effectively excludes bishops and laity from taking responsibility for decision making. Often people are happy to be part of a church without taking responsibility, but many of the more committed and active want to contribute. Excluding them from participation in authority leads to them feeling – correctly – that they are marginalised. It blocks the flow of energy in the Body of Christ. The periphery is cut off from the centre. In a human body if the blood stops flowing to the fingers they fall off. Franz König, Cardinal Archbishop of Vienna, wrote in 1999:

> In fact, however, *de facto* and not *de jure*, intentionally or unintentionally, the curial authorities working in conjunction with the pope have appropriated the tasks of the episcopal college. It is they who now carry out almost all of them.[1]

A tenth disadvantage is that Vatican II wanted a new balance between the papacy and the bishops. A minority opposed this.

1. 'My Vision of the Church of the Future', *The Tablet*, 7 March 1999, p 434, quoted by Kevin Dowling, op cit.

In the years since the council it seems as if the views of the minority have dominated. Given that it is the papacy which decides the limits of its own power this is not surprising. It raises serious questions about possible conflicts in magisterial teaching: the council, made up of the bishops and the pope, with its decrees approved by the pope is the most authoritative element of the magisterium. How is the church to deal with apparent tensions between popes and conciliar documents?

An eleventh disadvantage is that a monarchical papacy, given that the pope and the bishops are always male, is likely to reinforce and not challenge patriarchy.

A twelfth disadvantage is that there is a contradiction between the Vatican insisting on its authority over bishops in the area of doctrine but denying all liability when bishops fail to respond appropriately to abuse issues. So, in 2011 Bishop William Morris of Toowoomba diocese in Australia was removed from pastoral care by the Vatican. He said that this happened because he suggested that the church could help solve the problem of priest shortages by considering ordaining women and married men. Joseph Huang Bingzhang, was excommunicated in the same year for accepting ordination as a bishop in China's state-sanctioned Catholic church without Vatican approval. The Vatican cannot credibly claim hierarchical responsibility in these cases and deny it when the issue is abuse.

A thirteenth disadvantage is that increasing the centralised power of the papacy makes a negative impact on ecumenical relationships. One response to this may be: well that is tough but the reality is that the truth of the tradition requires a stronger papacy and other churches need to accept this. That view, however, takes no account of the desire of Our Lord for unity among his followers (John 17:23) or of serious theological arguments against a monarchical papacy. Nor does it take account of the call of the church to be catholic, or universal.

Many of the above disadvantages coincide with some of the causes of the abuse crisis: patriarchy, superiority, lack of accountability, deference and lack of transparency. We therefore face some questions and issues about our structures:

- Are we sure of the biblical basis of our structures? They have, naturally, developed since New Testament times.

In what ways are they now in keeping with the values of the New Testament?

- The tension between the goals of Vatican II and how the church has developed since needs to be faced anew
- Vatican II ended in 1965. That is a lifetime for people born since then. The council did not clarify the tensions between the powers of the papacy and the bishops. It did not set up structures to implement the value of collegiality which had been more prominent in previous eras.
- The council stressed that the church is made up of the People of God. But it did not work through the implications of this. As long as all authority is held by the ordained, lay people will remain passive, not active, members of the church. It is obvious that this was not the case in the early church – all the community participated in various decisions as we have seen. While church structures of today should not necessarily be the same as those of the early church because our needs are different we need some satisfactory explanation as to why lay people have been excluded from the exercise of authority.

Given this critique of present church structures, the gap between the values it reveals and those of the gospels, and the possible influence between the structures and the abuse crisis, what is the way forward for the church?

SECTION FIVE

Repentance and Hope?

CHAPTER ELEVEN

Repentance and Hope?

The response of many people to the abuse crisis has been to walk away from the church. One report suggested that in Germany alone 180,000 left the church in 2010.[1] Leaving the church in Germany is not a spur-of-the-moment decision: to do so one has to go to the local municipal authority and sign a form. The exodus is understandable but in the end I have chosen not to follow it.

People choose their church for a variety of reasons. Some of these are because of clear theological arguments, the witness of its members, because they were born into the church and it would be too threatening to leave, because they want to be free of institutional constraints and value individualism over community membership, because they know people in the church, and other reasons. Rowan Williams, the Archbishop of Canterbury, was tempted to join the Catholic Church at one stage, but allegedly decided not to do so because of papal infallibility. John Henry Newman joined the church because in his view it was the church with the strongest claim to be descended from the apostolic church.

Most people, myself included, will not decide about church membership on the basis of such clear and distinct ideas. What I can say is that the process of writing this book has steadied me in remaining in the Catholic Church, which in some ways is a surprising outcome, at least to me.

Part of this process involved getting in touch again with the love of God in the scriptures. In Chapter Four, I reflected on some of the passages that mean most to me. Of course the scriptures are available to people in other churches and much of my knowledge of them has been gleaned from dialogue with Protestants. It was Protestant reformers who re-emphasised the importance of the scriptures and pushed for them to be translated, moves resisted for many decades by Catholics. But recognising the gifts of other churches is not, in itself, a reason to change one's denomination.

---

1. *The Tablet*, 16 April 2011, p 32.

One principle of ecumenical relations is that one should always encourage people in other churches to probe the depths of their own tradition before encouraging them to join one's own church. If we followed that principle most of us would be long dead before we had exhausted the riches of our own tradition. The same principle applies when we consider leaving our own church. The principle does not rule out all moves between churches but it does recommend caution.

Writing this book has deepened my knowledge of both the good and the bad in the Catholic Church.

On the good side is the fact that much of my knowledge of God has been mediated through the church. This involved my early learning about God in my family, being brought to Mass and over the years developing a deep love for the Eucharist as a central way in which to experience the presence of Christ, the importance of the other sacraments, being taught how to pray, experiencing at times the silence of the presence of God, the theological training I received as a Jesuit, the call to peacemaking which is deeply important to the church, the universality of the church which is meant to transcend all national and cultural boundaries, the diversity that this implies, and the unity within that diversity – with all its limitations.

There is also the life and work of many lay people, both married and single, of parents, deacons, religious, priests, bishops, popes, teachers, community workers, youth workers, educators, retreat givers, chaplains, counsellors, carers, people who have given their lives to working against poverty at home and abroad, peace makers, ecumenists, theologians, writers, philosophers, astronomers and thinkers in other areas – the list could go on.

There is also the inspiration of the saints: Mary Magdalen, the first of the apostles, Augustine, Aquinas, Ignatius, Maximilian Kolbe, Dietrich Bonhoeffer, Gandhi, Martin Luther King, Paddy Doyle, John Clear, Michael Hurley, Liz Ryan, Pedro Arrupe, Eric and Ernest Gallagher, John Morrow, David Stevens. All of us have our own list. In my case some were married, Liz Ryan was a single parent and grandmother, others had no children. Some were not members of our modern Catholic Church: Magdalen, Augustine and Aquinas preceded the

Reformation. Bonhoeffer was Lutheran, Martin Luther King a Baptist, Ernest and Eric Gallagher Methodists, John Morrow and David Stevens Presbyterian, and Gandhi a Hindu. However, all had several things in common: they were sinners, they were loved by God, and they knew this. There is nothing surprising in an ecumenical list of saints: to be a Catholic is to be ecumenical and that in part means working with and finding inspiration from people in other churches and faiths.

The negatives, as we have seen, are strong: the patriarchy which emerged so early in the church, the clericalism which was linked to it and which is so opposed to the collegial involvement of the whole community that was present in the early church, the exclusion of lay people, originally in an effort to limit the power of strong local princes, the rift with the church of the East in 1054, which left the church breathing on one lung, the split with the Reformers in the sixteenth century which further weakened diversity and universality, the increasing centralisation and authoritarianism of the papacy from the mid-nineteenth century, the emergence of globalisation which deepened this process, the failure of the church to implement many of the calls of Vatican II, especially in the area of collegiality, the lack of respect for people of different sexual orientation, the exclusion of women, the lack of transparency and accountability, the Western European focus which does not take seriously enough the majority of church members who are from other areas, the limits imposed on ecumenical relationships, limits which show insufficient respect for the insights of theologians from different churches gleaned over one hundred years of work.

One could add to this list the terrible atrocities in which the church has been involved over the centuries, especially its support for slavery, the Crusades, and the contribution that Christians made to anti-semitism. The terrible response of the church to the suffering endured by abused children is one more example of the capacity of the church to act in ways utterly opposed to the love of its Founder.

So why do I choose to remain in the church? I think it is not because of a weighing of the plusses and minuses and finding that the benefits are greater. Nor, I hope, is it out of fear of the consequences of leaving, difficult though these would be.

Rather, it is a sense that God is at work in this church, corrupt though it is. Indeed, corruption can never block God. If it could do so then the incarnation would have been impossible.

In his *Spiritual Exercises* Ignatius of Loyola has a meditation in which he invites the retreatant to contemplate the Three Divine Persons in the Blessed Trinity looking down on the world and seeing so many sinning and thereby being separated from God and from each other. In the meditation the Three Persons take the sin of the world seriously. Sin is about hurting people wrongly either by omission or commission. All sin, as well as hurting people, hurts God. Yet the response of God was not to destroy people, as the writers of the Old Testament thought so often. Nor was it to force people to act with respect. Rather it was to hand over the Son into our power in a process which led to the cross.

On the cross Christ did not reject his own people who were butchering him. Rather he spoke on their behalf to the Father: 'Forgive them, for they know not what they do' (Lk 23:34). His commitment to his people, and to the people of the world was unconditional. It did not depend on their acting well.

This love of God does not in any way reduce the awfulness of sin or the anger of God at it. But it means that God does not walk away from the sinner, even when the sinner walks away from God. Rather, as Balthasar suggests in his meditation on Holy Saturday, God enters into Hades so as to be in solidarity with those who have separated themselves from God: although separated, they will now, through Christ, be connected to the Father.

As we have seen, the same theme occurs constantly in the Old Testament: the people grumble against God and turn to idolatry. God's anger flares against them, but in the end God – often persuaded by Moses and others – turns away from anger and back to a compassionate love. The people are called to repentance. They are punished for their sins. But God's love in the end triumphs. The sin of the people, disastrous though it has been in its consequences, is not fatal because the love of God is greater than their evil.

This reflection does not answer the question, why this church and not another? So behind it lies a belief that God is still at work in the Catholic Church and that this church is related, in however complex a way, to that group of Jews who first experienced Christ as being alive after the cross and began to tell others this extraordinary news. Of course God is at work in other churches and faiths, as the above list of saints shows, but should I leave the Catholic Church and join another because of the terrible list of negatives in our church? Other churches have their own difficulties and can often appear attractive to the outsider who has not experienced them.

I think the choice would be to leave the church if any of the following were true:

- That the Catholic Church is evil at its core and the response to the abuse revealed this.
- That the church is not connected with that early group who began to follow Christ.
- That the church in principle is irreformable.

I believe all these are false statements, although I am sometimes tempted to believe them.

The church is more, much more, than the response to abuse. That does not in any way lessen the horror of that response. It simply emphasises that God's love is greater than any evil. To say that the church is evil at its core is to miss this point.

Secondly, I believe that the Catholic Church, as is the case with many other Christian churches, is connected with the early church. Not only this, but Christ is present and working in the church. Further, the church is the Body of Christ. Christ is present in the world in many ways: one of the main ways is through the church. The scandal of division, the response to abuse and the other faults of the church make this more difficult to see but it does not make it untrue.

The third statement, that the church is irreformable, is also tempting, but to accept it one would need to ignore history. History shows that everything changes. We have seen how the church has changed over the centuries. Much of that has been for the good. The church now opposes slavery and capital punishment in almost all cases (it would be better if its opposition was absolute). It has changed profoundly, if insufficiently, in its relationships with other churches. Pressure is increasing for reform in the areas of patriarchy and authoritarianism, and new structures have been introduced, however slowly, in which lay people are at least consulted, if not empowered. So the church is certainly not irreformable in principle. But for those working for reform the struggle is long and hard, and at times it is easy to lose heart.

However, if we decide to stay in the church and if we also see the task of the church as being the sign of the presence of God in the world, then we must work to change the church. What changes, therefore, are needed? The first is to repent.

Repentance

The Christian message is clear that the proper response to wrongdoing is repentance. As a church we need to repent for our institutional response to the abuse. In part this involves saying 'Sorry' and meaning it. It also means making a firm purpose of amendment, and accepting just punishment.

Church leaders have said 'Sorry' and meant it but conveying this takes time. It is a process. It needs words and actions. It needs public expression. An Augustinian priest, Fr Michael Mernagh, walked from Cobh in Ireland to Dublin in 2009 – about one hundred and sixty miles – as an attempt to do this. There were also many initiatives in local parishes and there were quiet, unpublicised acts of penance by some clergy and laity, for example in doing pilgrimages on Lough Derg. We need other imaginative, creative images to communicate our shame, our horror at abuse and other wrongs, and our commitment to change.

Repentance includes restitution. We cannot make good the harm done, but it gives some benefits to those who have been abused. Money will not heal people, but it will provide some services such as counselling or health insurance. Many religious congregations and dioceses have already given large sums but their funds are limited. For this reason, and because the state itself is in part corporately responsible for the abuse, the state will have to bear the greater burden of costs. This comment is not meant to diminish the church's responsibility. It simply faces the fact that assets are limited. There is also a need for state-sponsored inquiries in Northern Ireland and to give people who have been abused there the same recognition as those in the Republic of Ireland.

Repentance also means accepting appropriate punishment. For clergy and religious this may mean accepting the understandable fury of people at what the institution has done. Priests and religious are corporately connected to the church's response. It is not surprising if we are blamed more than others, given that for so long we belonged to a system in which priests and religious were seen as being the whole church – despite Vatican II's emphasis on the People of God.

The role of papacy in the church's repentance
The Pope has an important role to play in expressing the repentance of the whole church, as a representative of both the wider Roman Catholic community and of the papal bureaucracy that like so many other parts of the church responded badly to abuse. A papal visit to Ireland has been discussed. Many see it as undesirable because they think it would be similar to the last visit by John Paul II. Yet a pilgrimage of repentance would be quite different. What might this look like? A Pope praying on his knees at some of the institutions examined by Ryan? A Pope showing not only by what he said, but by how he said it, that he and the church are deeply repentant? A Pope backing up such repentance with concrete actions such as a significant contribution to a fund for those who were abused?

Papal visits to Australia, the US and Great Britain were received much better than might have been expected, given prior publicity. In part this was because people got close up views of Pope Benedict acting in a personal, pastoral way. That changed the previous image many had of him. It is also noteworthy that during many of these visits the Pope met with a group of people who had been abused and they seemed to have been helped by the meetings, although obviously in each case the individuals were carefully selected.

Corporate repentance is different from individual repentance
There is a difficulty in speaking about corporate repentance, similar to that of speaking about corporate involvement. People can only say 'Sorry' for wrong they have done. They cannot say 'Sorry' for wrong in which they played no part. So I can regret the IRA campaign in Northern Ireland because it was immoral. I cannot personally say sorry for it because I did not take part in it.

Corporate guilt does not imply personal guilt. It is the institution, not the individuals that is guilty. So is it appropriate for the church as an institution to repent? Yes, because it is corporately guilty. Individual guilt is a separate issue and each of us should ask if we did things that allowed abuse to continue or failed to do things that might have stopped it.

Asking for forgiveness?

Many church leaders have called on people who were abused to forgive the church. Some have argued in favour of this on the grounds that it empowers those who were abused: they are given a choice, which is precisely what they lacked when they were abused. However, there is a strong argument against asking for forgiveness: to do so puts a moral burden on those who suffered. They have the choice to move towards offering forgiveness or not. That is a long painful journey for most, with many stages on the way.[1] Asking for forgiveness can put the wrongdoer on the high moral ground and make moral demands on the person wronged. It seems wiser for the church to focus instead on repentance rather than adding burdens to those who have been wronged.

Repentance also means a commitment to reform. I have argued in this book that there is a connection between current church structures and the response to the abuse because aspects of the structures parallel elements which emerged in the response to abuse: patriarchy, superiority, lack of accountability and transparency, deference, and lack of diversity. Repentance therefore means changing our structures so that these elements are no longer present.

Repentance also means getting back to our vision, coming back to the Way of the Lord. In our survey of the scriptures, we found values such as love, respect, acceptance of diversity and a place for women. These are the very opposite of the values shown in the bad response to abuse. If, then, we want to repent of our church's response to child abuse, we need to address our structures and the values which underlie them.

---

1. Brian Lennon SJ, *So You Can't Forgive*, Columba, 2009, pp 15-19.

STRUCTURAL REFORM

A church of the People of God?

Many church members have experience of other movements such as Trades Unions or political parties in which they – both men and women – had a voice. They elected members to committees or were themselves elected. They made an impact on the organisation. They were taken seriously. That happens also in some parishes and dioceses. But the law and practice of the church currently means that inclusion of lay people, both men and women, is dependent on the vision and commitment of individual priests and bishops. We need a church where this is not the case, where the life and energy of the people flows irrespective of who is the priest or bishop. We cannot have that without empowering the laity.

As we have seen, the exclusion of laity from authority in the church is historically recent: formally it only happened with the most recent *Code of Canon Law* in 1983. There were good reasons for excluding the laity at times in the past: it was an effort to free the church from dominance by lay kings, emperors and lords. That historical context has changed. We need a new code which involves lay people. To underpin this we need a new theology of the church. For that we need a new council.

A central insight of Vatican II was the need for the church to develop a new focus on the People of God. The council members did not spell out in detail what that meant but they were clear that the primary status of each member of the church was as a member of the people, not one of being a pope, bishop, priest, deacon or lay person.

Secondly, Vatican II called for a new re-balancing between the centre and periphery, between pope and bishops, in the church.

Vatican II ended a long time ago but its hopes have not been realised: the vision of the minority, rejected at the council, not that vision of the majority, has since been implemented. There is a need to return to the vision of the council. But doing so alone is insufficient. We now need to spell out what focusing on the People of God means in concrete structures: are we going to exclude women from government forever in the church both by denying them ordination and by excluding the non-ordained from government? We cannot do so and at the same time maintain that we are repenting of patriarchy, a central element in the response to abuse. Similarly, it is difficult to see how we can maintain the monarchical trappings of the papacy which have increased since the nineteenth century while also committing ourselves to accountability, transparency and a lack of superiority.

It would be foolish to expect a change of structures to be a panacea for the church's problems. Other churches, with arguably more appropriate structures than ours, have plenty of problems of their own. Yet changing our structures can help remove blocks to reform. It can engage all the members of the church in the life of the church instead of keeping them as objects of male, clerical decisions.

Vatican II pointed in the direction of a new church in which all the members, irrespective of their gender, could contribute much more deeply to the life of the church. Our call to follow Christ, to be witnesses to the love of God for the world, to repent for the wrongs our church has done to children, all impel us to seek deep reform.

New oversight
There is a need for new authority structures within the church. One example: it is not entirely clear to me where the balance of authority lies between a child protection office appointed by all the bishops of a country or region and that of a local bishop. The powers of a bishop within his diocese are very great within canon law, the powers of a bishops' conference less so. This is partly due to the increased centralisation since Vatican II: the papacy did not want regional conferences to balance its own authority. There has been a welcome change in that a bishop who refuses to respond appropriately to a national child protection officer is likely to face civil legal consequences. But what changes in canon law are also needed?

Secondly, a parish priest is required by canon law to appoint a finance committee which includes at least four lay people. The powers of these committees are laid out in canon 537. How many lay people know this? How many help to exercise oversight in the area of finance?

Lay people need greater decision-making powers in the church, but they also need to be aware of the powers that they already have.

Diversity

The church needs to examine its structures in regard to diversity. This includes changing the dominance of the church by the papal civil service, and embracing the church's vocation to be truly a church of the world. It means taking ecumenism much more seriously and giving people from other churches a greater role in vetting the impact of church statements and actions on ecumenical relations. And it means addressing the issue of marginalised groups in the church, such as those of different sexual orientation who feel excluded by the church's teaching.

How will the church change?

Christ works in the church through grace. Grace is the love of God coming into contact with fallible human beings. Many times I wish Christ would get on with it and change things more quickly. But that is a two-fold temptation: it is asking Christ to be a magician, a role he rejected. Secondly it is asking him to impose my views on the world, which might not always be a good idea.

The church is called to be a sign of the presence of God's love in the world. At the root of this lies a call: the call of Christ to each human person to engage with his world and to make the church, his Body, a real sign of his love.

The first task for each of us is to get in touch with that call. That is not easy. We can be discouraged by the things that are wrong, feel undermined by secularism, discouraged by the slowness of change. That is why the need is so great first to get in touch with the call of Christ. Without that we have no chance of responding well. Either we will give up or we will act out of the bad spirit in which we impose our will in exactly the same authoritarian manner that we criticise in others.

To get in touch with Christ's call we need prayer. Some of this involves time on our own in which we face the silence of God. Only in that stillness will some of the noise of our world and our false selves quieten down and only then will we be able to hear more deeply. We also need prayer with others to sense the unity that we can have even with people with whom we disagree deeply.

Secondly, to change the church we need something like the dialogue that was discussed earlier: an attempt to listen to each other – not to agree, but to understand why it is that we hold different views. Why are some people passionately opposed to the ordination of women? Why do others find such views incomprehensible except as part of prejudice? Dialogue is needed with those with whom we disagree deeply, not with like-minded people.

Thirdly, we need to understand how big organisations work. It is not enough to have good people in key positions. Good people in a bad organisation will end up colluding in bad decisions. The response to abuse is one glaring example of this. The church has all the hallmarks of any other big organisation. The dynamics of large organisations differ from those of small groups. There is a role for small groups, but also for intelligent application of what has been learnt about large organisations.

Fourthly, change will only come about with effective lobbying and political action. This will not happen without organised campaigns by lay people, religious and clergy. All movements for change happen because varieties of groups, young and old, begin to ask questions, meet together, analyse problems, come up with strategies for change and implement them.

An example is the change brought about by the neo-cons in the US. They set up think tanks, analysed international relations, concluded that liberalism was behind many of the world's problems, got editors and presenters into key positions in talk radio shows and other media, had their people elected to key political posts, and eventually got George Bush Jnr elected as President of the US. That led in turn to disastrous decisions about the environment, the invasion of Iraq and Afghanistan and the deaths of thousands of people. It was a movement that began in the 1950s and came to fruition after 2000.

If a group like the neo-Cons can organise themselves so well, albeit for disastrous purposes, can Catholics, together with people from other churches, not organise themselves to bring the church closer to the vision Christ had for it?

Fifthly, change will only happen with international co-operation. A feature of the abuse crisis was the way other countries looked on and thanked God that they were not involved as it emerged elsewhere. But of course they were involved and one of the failures of the Vatican was in not making this clear. People who are unhappy with the way the church is in one country need to work with others because the church is an international body. Without international co-operation child protection protocols will not be in place all over the world as they need to be.

Sixthly, some groups need to focus on finance. Finance can sometimes concentrate minds when theological discussion fails. How are church funds being used? Who is being paid, how much and why? How are the assets of the Vatican bank used and invested? These are church funds. They belong to the People of God. They are to be used for the spread of Christ's word. We need to ask by what values and policies they are being administered and how the administrators are accountable.

Seventhly, change needs to be led for the most part by lay people. Bishops and priests have also a role, but because of the repression of criticism by the Vatican we are more curtailed in our freedom. For lay people to take a lead they need theological education. Already this has happened with many lay people being far more qualified than clergy. But more is needed because theological understanding as well as prayer needs to underpin arguments for change. The church will not reform if lay people sit back and wait for it to happen.

Healing for those who were abused

While vindication, punishment, restitution, and counselling can help, healing in the end has to come from within. For many that is a long and deeply painful journey.

Those who were abused should not be defined by their abuse: they have other identities. The move towards healing seems to coincide with slowly reaching a place in which they define themselves no longer as only victims but also as husbands or fathers, wives or mothers, who were abused as children. The abuse becomes one of many important aspects of their lives rather than the only one.

Some priests and religious have been abused. These are in a double role: they have been abused, and at the same time are members of institutions that have done wrong. This shows something of the complexity of the issue.

Dealing with those who were abused

Abuse is a crime. Most crime in Ireland, North and South, is punished by prison. Prison is necessary to protect society from some criminals, but, as can be seen by international compar-isons, it is a costly and often ineffective approach if the person convicted is no longer a danger to society. It is incorrect to as-sume that all who are convicted of abuse do not reform. The un-derstandable anger against abuse can block people from ac-cepting this. The result is that all who abuse are treated the same. This does not help child protection. A more useful ap-proach would focus firstly on child protection, secondly on re-form of the person who abused, and thirdly on punishment. This would produce better outcomes in all three areas.

People who have abused remain human beings and sons and daughters of God and brothers and sisters of Christ. There is no wrong that cannot be forgiven by God's grace, provided the sin-ner repents.

A new ecumenical council?

Change in structures in the Catholic Church involves a mixture of doctrinal development, changes in canon law, and new deci-sion-making structures. Effectively this needs a new ecumenical council.

A council is also needed because the cultural and political context in which the church operates has changed dramatically since Vatican II in 1965. The church is now dominated by non-Europeans, the Berlin Wall has fallen, the weaknesses of untram-melled capitalism have been exposed, post-modernism has raised challenging questions about faith, scientific methods have greatly increased our understanding of the scriptures, the ecu-menical movement has dramatically changed relations between churches. In particular a feminist understanding has changed gender relations.

These changes are so vast that we need a council to discern how the church should respond to the modern world – one of the major themes of Vatican II. If, instead of this, a council was called to shore up the church's defences against the modern world it would be a disaster.

We will not have a new council without much movement in local churches. Such movement is needed for the Body of Christ to awaken. A sign of that might be many local synods, something that was an aspect of the church for the first millennium and still is in the Orthodox and Reformed churches, but which has been largely lost in the Latin, Western church.

All the above are parts of the way that the church needs to repent. However, repentance by the church cannot heal those who have been abused.

Conclusion

On 17 November 2010 the Archbishop of Canterbury and Leader of the Anglican Communion, Rowan Williams, gave an important address on the theme 'Towards a new stage of ecumenical dialogue'.[1] The occasion was the fiftieth anniversary of the Pontifical Council for Promoting Christian Unity. It is an appropriate place to end these reflections because in his remarks the archbishop outlined a theological basis which could guide us within the Catholic Church as we face the task of reform.

He pointed to three themes in the New Testament which help us understand the unity that God wants between divided churches. The first of these was unity in Jesus Christ with God the Father. This is about being caught up in the relationships of the Father, the Son and the Holy Spirit. It is about praying to God Our Father – 'Abba' or 'Daddy' was the term of intimacy used by Jesus. It is about us becoming adopted children of God and taking on the mind of Christ.

Because of this unity with God the second theme is our unity with each other. This is about loving our sisters and brothers. In part this means being emptied of self-concern, as Christ was.

The third theme is being called to be witnesses of Christ's love.

On foot of these themes Rowan Williams argues that 'the visible concrete life of the church must be a life that expresses and realises our standing in Christ': our life must be one of communion in the Holy Trinity. He sees the Eucharist as the place above all where the prayer of Christ becomes our prayer 'and the life of Christ becomes our life in the sacramental tokens of his body and blood ... A church which is serious about unity with Christ, is a church which is devoted to growing and nourishing that life of prayer which is Christ's life in us'.

---

1. 'Address at 50th anniversary of the Pontifical Council for Promoting Christian Unity', Vatican City, 17 November 2010.

Secondly, the Eucharist impels us to serve Christ's brothers and sisters (which includes all the people of the world).

Thirdly, the church, in union with the apostles, must witness to the cross and resurrection. Part of this involves the church being held to account 'by the agreed doctrinal discernment of the whole body'. In other words, the whole body – in which he includes divided churches – needs to be part of the discernment of true doctrine.

Rowan Williams was speaking about ecumenical relationships, especially between the Church of Rome and the Anglican Communion. But the three themes he mentions – being caught up in the love of the Trinity, service of each other, and witnessing to the cross and resurrection of Christ in ways that involve Christians from many churches – are key themes that a reforming church needs to highlight. Obviously, if members of divided churches need to be included in the discernment of doctrine, so also do lay Christians within the Catholic Church.

Rowan Williams is under no illusions about how difficult it is to reform the church – he has been an ecumenist almost all his life – especially in the area of structures of authority. But he sees it as essential to do this because: '[I]f we want to know that it is Christ we are talking about, in his death and resurrection, the question of unity with the apostolic witness is not a matter of indifference.' So he sees it as worthwhile to continue discussions about church structures, including the role of the Bishop of Rome.

Hope

The Catholic church after the revelations about the response to abuse is in desolation. So we should be. The organisation, and many individuals, have sinned grievously. That leads to shame, anger, division, depression and hopelessness among many priests and lay people. The way out of a sinful situation is through repentance. Repentance, in the Christian vision, leads to hope.

Hope is not the same as optimism. I do not know if the church will respond to the need for new structures. I do know it will change because history shows it is changing all the time. Whether that change will be good or bad remains to be seen.

At the end of the journey of writing this book, however, I have hope. It is a hope tinged, as always, with doubt. But the Christian story is about a God who loved the world so much that the First Person of the Holy Trinity handed over the Son to us out of love for us. The love of God has in the past overcome evil in organisations and within each of us and will do so again in the future. The heritage we have received is too rich for us to let it go.

Repentance can turn us from a reactive, depressed group into one that has re-focused on our values, on where we came from, on the story of Christ who reveals God to us. Repentance looks to the past by confessing our communal and individual guilt. It looks to the present by asking in what way wrong is continuing today. But it also looks to the future by asking what we need to do in order to be true to our calling. That can free us.

We will continue to face many difficulties, although they will be nothing compared to the pain faced by those abandoned by the church when they were abused. Those difficulties represent new challenges to implement our call to be the presence of God in the world. Lay people, deacons, priests, bishops, and popes, are called to be that presence of God in the world. We can only do this in a church which has a new vision, new structures in which each can play a role, and one that works together with our brothers and sisters in other Christian churches.

Our call is not to make the church into our ideal vision of it. Rather we are called together to witness to the presence of the love of God in the world. The issue then is not the result – that lies in the hands of God – but rather how committed we are in our life, our work, our repentance and our celebration of God's gifts to us, to making visible that love of God.

In this context, tempting though it is to walk away from an in-stitution that is so flawed, the way forward may be to plumb the depths of our own tradition, to get in touch again with the vision of so many of our ancestors, to call our church from sin to life, and to do so with the help and challenge of Christians in other churches and people of good will in other faiths and none.

All of us who believe in God, whatever about our doubts, and all of us who have experienced Christ, have been given a deep gift. That gift is not meant to be enjoyed alone. Of its very nature we are called by it to be part of the church, a church which is wider than the Catholic Church. We are also called to do what we can, despite our sins and failings, to help the church fulfil our vocation to be a sign of the presence of Christ in the world.

That presence, if it is to reflect the life of Christ, needs to enshrine qualities of respect for all human beings. In turn that makes it imperative to struggle against the sins of patriarchy, domination, superiority, deference, lack of transparency and accountability, and to struggle for the values of compassion, justice, inclusiveness, repentance and forgiveness.

The treatment of those who were abused is the very opposite of the values to which Christ calls us. Our church has sinned grievously. We need to repent and turn away from wrongdoing. But we can also be assured that the grace of Christ is always there for the repentant sinner and that Christ cannot abandon his own Body. If we turn towards Christ we too can still be part of that Body.

Hope needs action

The abuse crisis does not of itself make it impossible to believe in God, unless we believe it is impossible for God to exist in a context of sin. What it can do is discourage us so much that we give up searching for God or walk away from the church. People who want a church with greater respect for persons can also be discouraged after years of failure. Yet if those who believe that the church is meant to be the sign of the presence of God in the world give up the task of making this a reality it will not happen.

During the Industrial Revolution workers organised themselves in a hard struggle that eventually led to more just labour relations, at least in some parts of the world. In Ireland, the 19th century struggle against landlords was also eventually successful because people organised themselves into the Land League. Equality for women, outside the church, has improved since the 1950s, because of the feminist movement and the work of Trade Unionists, among others. The struggle of the solidarity movement in Poland, supported especially by John Paul II, was one of the important elements in the fall of the Soviet Union, leading to greater freedom for many. Paradoxically, many of these movements were supported by Catholic church leaders and members while at the same time the church itself was becoming increasingly authoritarian and made no moves towards equality for women or lay people within it.

As an institution the church is subject to the same dynamics as other institutions. It will change when there are sufficient focused campaigns for a justice within the church that parallels the calls for justice outside the church based on Catholic Social Teaching. In the church's case these campaigns need to take place within the context of scripture and tradition.

The church will not change because of pious hopes. So this book ends with a question for all Catholics: what can we do to make the church become the sign of the presence of God in the world?

This question is addressed in a special way to lay people. The hierarchical church has often acted in a repressive way towards ordained clergy and religious. It has less power to do so towards laity. So, how can lay people organise themselves (and it must be a group – individuals tend to be powerless when alone) so as to change the institution of the church?

One suggestion is to focus on canon 129. This is one of the church laws that excludes lay people from the exercise of significant authority in the church. If we change it clericalism will decline and accountability could be improved. If lay people begin to exercise a degree of authority this could open the door to changes in the role of women in the church.

Repentance leads to hope and hope leads to action. What action do you need to take?